The Nordic Nations in the
New Western Security Regime

The Nordic
Nations in the
New Western
Security Regime

Ingemar Dörfer

WW *Published by The Woodrow Wilson Center Press*
Distributed by The Johns Hopkins University Press

Woodrow Wilson Center Special Studies

The Woodrow Wilson Center Press
Editorial Offices
370 L'Enfant Promenade, S.W.
Suite 704
Washington, D.C. 20024-2518 U.S.A.
telephone 202-287-3000, ext. 218

Distributed by
The Johns Hopkins University Press
2715 N. Charles Street
Baltimore, Maryland 21211
order department telephone 1-800-537-5487

Library of Congress Cataloging-in-Publication Data

Dörfer, Ingemar.
    The Nordic nations in the New Western Security Regime.
        p.   cm. — (Woodrow Wilson Center special studies)
    Includes bibliographical references and index.
    ISBN 0-943875-83-8 (alk. paper.) — ISBN 0-943875-82-X (pbk. :
alk. paper)
      1. National security—Scandinavia.   2. Scandinavia—Defenses.
3. North Atlantic Treaty Organization.   I. Series.
UA646.7.D67   1997
355'.033048—dc21   97-8532
                                               CIP

The Woodrow Wilson International Center for Scholars

The Center is the living memorial of the United States of America to the nation's twenty-eighth president, Woodrow Wilson. Congress established the Woodrow Wilson Center in 1968 as an international institute for advanced study, "symbolizing and strengthening the fruitful relationship between the world of learning and the world of public affairs." The Center opened in 1970 under its own board of trustees.

Woodrow Wilson Center Special Studies

The work of the Center's Fellows, Guest Scholars, and staff—and presentations and discussions at the Center's conferences, seminars, and colloquia—often deserve timely circulation as contributions to public understanding of issues of national and international importance. The Woodrow Wilson Center Special Studies series is intended to make such materials available by the Woodrow Wilson Center Press to interested scholars, practitioners, and other readers. In all its activities, the Woodrow Wilson Center is a nonprofit, nonpartisan organization, supported financially by annual appropriations from the U.S. Congress, and by the contributions of foundations, corporations, and individuals. Conclusions or opinions expressed in Center publications and programs are those of the authors and speakers and do not necessarily reflect the views of the Center's staff, Fellows, trustees, advisory groups, or any individuals or organizations that provide financial support to the Center.

For Joanne

Contents

Maps

Tables

Abbreviations

ACV	Armored Combat Vehicle
AFCENT	Allied Forces Central Europe (NATO)
AFNORTHWEST	Allied Forces Northwestern Europe (NATO)
AMF	Allied Command Europe Mobile Force (NATO)
AMRAAM	Advanced medium range air to air missile
ARRC	Allied Command Europe Rapid Reaction Corps (NATO)
AWACS	Advanced Warning and Control System (NATO)
BALTBAT	Baltic Peacekeeping Battalion
BAOR	British Army of the Rhine
BWC	Biological Weapons Convention
C^3I	Command, Control, Communications, and Intelligence
CASTBE	Canadian Air Sea Transportable Brigade Group
CFE	Conventional Forces in Europe
CFSP	Common Foreign and Security Policy (EU)
CINCENT	Commander in Chief Allied Forces Central Europe (NATO)
CINCNORTH	Commander in Chief Allied Forces Northern Europe (NATO)
CJTF	Combined Joint Task Forces (NATO)
COB	Co-located Operating Base (NATO)
DIB	Danish International Brigade
EC	European Community
EU	European Union
ICBM	Intercontinental Ballistic Missile
IFF	Identification Friend Foe
IFOR	Implementation Force (for Bosnia)

IGC	Intergovernmental Conference (EU)
IPP	Individual Partnership Program (NATO)
ISR	Intelligence Collection Surveillance and Reconnaisance
JAS	Swedish multipurpose combat aircraft
LANDJUT	Allied Land forces Jutland
MBT	Main battle tank
MIRV	Multiple Independent Re-entry Vehicle
NAC	North Atlantic Council (NATO)
NACC	North Atlantic Cooperation Council (NATO)
NAL MAGTF	Norway Airlanded Marine Air Ground Task Force (U.S.)
NATO	North Atlantic Treaty Organization
NAVNORTHWEST	Naval Forces Northwestern Europe (NATO)
NORDBAT	Nordic Peacekeeping Battalion (in the former Yugoslavia)
OSCE	Organization for Security and Cooperation in Europe
PARP	Planning and Review Process (NATO)
PFP	Partnership for Peace (NATO)
PSC	Principal Subordinate Command (NATO)
SACEUR	Supreme Allied Commander Europe (NATO)
SACLANT	Supreme Allied Commander Atlantic (NATO)
SFOR	Stabilization Force (for Bosnia)
SHAPE	Supreme Headquarters Allied Powers Europe
SLBM	Submarine-Launched Ballistic Missile
SLOCS	Sea lines of communications
SOP	Standard Operating Procedures (NATO)
STANAG	Standardization agreement
START	Strategic Arms Reduction Talks
TLE	Treaty limited equipment
UNPROFOR	United Nations Protection Force (in the former Yugoslavia)
WEAG	Western European Armaments Group
WEU	Western European Union
WMD	Weapons of Mass Destruction
WWII	World War II

Acknowledgments

This study resulted from the insight that the thinking of many Scandinavians, and in particular Swedes, had not adjusted to the new security situation in Europe after the cold war. In the fall of 1994, I persuaded Mats Johansson, then director of the Swedish free market think tank and publishing house *Timbro* that a book on the subject would be appropriate. Although *Timbro* and the Swedish Ministry for Foreign Affairs contributed generous seed money, it was clear to me that the thinking and writing that went into the study should be conducted away from the Scandinavian milieu. Uwe Nerlich invited me to spend the spring of 1995 as a guest scholar at the *Stiftung Wissenschaft und Politik* in Ebenhausen and Samuel F. Wells, Jr., encouraged me to be a guest scholar at the Woodrow Wilson International Center for Scholars in Washington, D.C., the same fall. My thanks go to them both as well as the directors Michael Stürmer and Charles Blitzer and the splendid staffs of these two venerable institutions. It was a special pleasure to revisit the Woodrow Wilson Center after seventeen years.

An in-house condensed version of this study was issued at the *Stiftung Wissenschaft und Politik* in February 1997, and I want to thank Peer Lange, Christine Kirstein, and Gisela Helms, and their staff for the special effort that went into this production. At the Woodrow Wilson Center Press, I thank the entire staff and in particular Joseph Brinley, Jr., Robert A. Poarch, and Carolee Belkin Walker. Many friends and colleagues who shall remain unnamed offered illuminating comments on the manuscript along the way.

The Swedish Defense Research Establishment, as often in the past, supported the effort financially and intellectually all along, and I thank Jan Foghelin who made it possible and my assistant Maria Edholm who transmitted my typewritten pages onto computer disks, both English and Swedish. The Swedish version published by *Timbro* in October 1996 under the title *Sverige är inte neutralt längre* was much facilitated by the editing of Cecilia Brinck.

The opinions expressed here are mine alone.

Summary

All Nordic nations have now joined the Western security regime led by the United States and have shown their willingness to use military force in that pursuit if necessary. Russia remains the sole security threat to these nations, and it is imperative that America remain in Europe and as the leader of NATO, the only viable defense organization of the West. To sustain meager American interest in Scandinavia and the Baltic states, Finland and Sweden should join NATO, thereby also supporting the Baltic states, which will not be able to join NATO in this century.

This study begins by explaining why there is so little international interest in Nordic security (they are not part of the NATO expansion debate) contrasting that lack of interest with the West's unreasonable expectations that the Nordic nations should handle Baltic security. Neither Finland nor Sweden is willing to act in the Baltics without the participation of the Western powers. Contrary to American, British, and German wishes, Finland and Sweden do not want to form a regional security group. Of the four international security institutions relevant to Europe, the UN and the OSCE are in decline, whereas the EU and NATO are more important than ever before. Finland and Sweden, traditional strong supporters of the UN and the OSCE, are moving toward and increasingly relying on the EU and NATO.

The second part of this study analyzes security resources of the North and the roles of the important Western friends—the United Kingdom, Germany, and the United States—in Nordic security. The Nordic nations have moved from the PFP via CJTFs to IFOR exactly like the Central European nations attempting to join NATO. Thus they have de facto positioned themselves for NATO membership.

The third part of this study shows how this membership could come about. Several NATO enlargement studies are discussed and applied to the Nordic nations. Since Poland is likely to join NATO soon, the implications of Polish membership are also studied. Sweden and Finland will not be able to slip into NATO unobtrusively as they slipped into the EU; a clear-cut decision must be made, since simple cooperation will not automatically bring membership. The Swedish public may have difficulty acknowledging the Swedish postwar history of secret cooperation with the West and may consider NATO as less of a collective security organization and more as a venue for participating in Petersberg operations. Finland will join NATO if the security establishment declares that it should and it will likely decide once Poland has joined. Because of the undefined relationship between the WEU and NATO, the best way for the once-neutral members of the EU to join the Western security community is by joining NATO. Since they could not stay out of a modern war in Northern Europe, since they now participate in most European security operations, and since they fit perfectly under the American information umbrella, NATO membership is the logical outcome of their actions since the cold war ended.

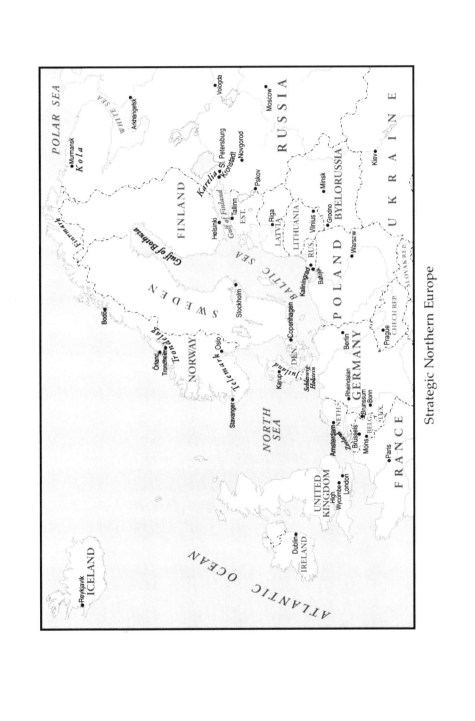

Strategic Northern Europe

Introduction

In May 1995 the Swedish Parliamentary Defense Commission published a report on Sweden's position in Europe and in the world. In this report, the aims of Sweden's security policy are formulated:

> The ultimate objective of Swedish security policy is to preserve the freedom and independence of our nation. Our goal is thus to secure our freedom of action, in all situations, and in forms that we ourselves choose, to ensure that we—as a nation and in cooperation—are able to further develop our society. Our security has both a national and an international dimension.
>
> *Nationally* we shall be able to confront military threats that directly affect Sweden. The most difficult amongst these would be an armed attack against our national freedom and independence. We shall also prevent and deal with situations which, while not threatening the freedom and independence of Sweden, could lead to serious tensions in or risks to our society.
>
> *Internationally* we shall, in cooperation with other countries, participate actively in different types of peace-keeping and humanitarian missions. In this quest for common security, we pursue our traditional policy within the UN, for peace and disarmament and for democratic, social, eco-

1

nomic and ecological development. We shall also cooperate internationally to prevent and deal with non-military threats and tensions.[1]

A number of paragraphs in the commission's report indicate suitable means for achieving these goals. The paragraph dealing with the prospects of membership in the North Atlantic Treaty Organization (NATO) reads, "Sweden's policy for military non-alignment remains unchanged. Swedish membership in NATO or the [Western European Union] would neither benefit Swedish security interests, nor [enhance] stability in our part of the world. Consequently it is fundamental for Sweden's security that our total defence maintains a long-term capability to contribute to regional stability and to confront possible threats against our nation."[2] Likewise, the Finnish Council of State maintained in its report to Parliament in June 1995, that "the aim of Finland's foreign and security policy is to ensure a secure future for the Finnish nation in a world of peace, cooperation and deepening integration. Finland promotes broad international interaction and works as a member of the European Union to strengthen [the] unity of the continent. As a member of the Council of Europe, Finland will work to consolidate democratic security. Finland's main objective is to expand cooperation and maintain a stable situation in northern Europe and the Baltic Sea region. Finland will further this goal best by remaining outside military alliances and by maintaining an independent defence."[3] The conclusions of both these reports are political statements, acts of faith based on consensus rather than analysis.

This study does not deal with political language. Much time has been spent fine-tuning statements that have been designed to show that the policies of the nations involved have changed. Much time has also been spent interpreting these signals—to be sure, more time inside the nations under study than outside. This study deals with the evolving structure of the post–cold war security situation in Europe, the dynamics of its institutions, and its impact on the nations under study. In this area deeds, not words, count, and the efforts of Nordic diplomats to square the circle have been directed mostly to their domestic audiences.[4] This study is about high politics in the traditional military-political sense. Despite the new security agenda featuring environmental security and transregional politics,[5] in the end traditional high politics will decide the fate of the Nordic nations.

Despite "the false promise of institutions,"[6] I believe that NATO and the European Union (EU) will be critical to the national security of these states.

Rather than using the government statements as a point of departure, then, I shall use two propositions from former National Security Council aide Philip Zelikow's brilliant essay "The Masque of Institutions":

> Since 1991, the most important issue of European security has been whether Russia and the states of East-Central Europe will become part of the hierarchy of Western political, economic and military power led by the United States, Germany, the UK and France. Will Russia and its neighbors accept this hierarchy and what it represents, or reject it, seeking a new political, economic and cultural identity out of the very fact of this rejection? The answer to this question is likely to be determined mainly by domestic political and economic developments in Russia and the other new democracies in Europe. The answer will not be determined by whether these countries are or are not members in one or another international institution, with the possible exception of the European Union.
>
> The second most important issue in European security since 1991 has been whether military power will be readied or employed to influence political developments in or near Europe, especially where the interests of the great powers are not fully engaged. This question will be answered by the way the United States and its European allies define and pursue their national interests in the particular disputes that arise. Only governments and their polities are politically and morally accountable for its use.[7]

For the purpose of this study I substitute "the Nordic nations"—namely, Sweden, Finland, Norway, Denmark, and Iceland—for "Russia and the states of East-Central Europe." Since Iceland is an Atlantic nation outside the EU, I have not included Iceland in this book. Within a Western Europe that already meets the criteria of a pluralistic security community—a group of nations among whom war is unthinkable[8]—the Nordic nations form an even more secure subcommunity. I am also interested in the three Baltic states—Estonia, Latvia, and Lithuania—since their conduct and fate will influence the national security situation in the Baltic region. Rather than inquire what they *say*, however, I am interested in what they *do*: Do they want to be part of the Western security regime? and Do they want to employ military power in the pursuit of their national interest?

This study is based on certain assumptions that should be made explicit: First, public opinion on national security is fickle in Northern Europe. Second, Russia is the main security problem for the North and will remain so. Third, the United States will maintain a significant presence in Europe. And fourth, the traditional defense of Western Europe will be handled by NATO.

Political Opinion in the North

Since the end of the cold war, the erratic nature of public opinion in Northern Europe has been shown again and again. Governments that have disregarded the opinion of their people have lived to regret it. At the same time it has been relatively easy to rally public opinion around fundamental shifts in policy when a determined effort has gone into presenting the policy to the public.

In Sweden in October 1990, the government and the Social Democratic party abruptly changed their decision not to join the European Community (EC). Economic realities dictated this reversal; what had been impossible in September was feasible just one month later. Yet sixty years of indoctrination had its price. Throughout the government campaign to join the EU the issue of foreign policy and national security was put on the back burner, lest the public raise uncomfortable questions. Nevertheless, the referendum of November 1994 showed the thinnest of margins for joining. Ever since the decision to join, opinion polls, as well as the elections to the European Parliament in September 1995, have consistently shown that a majority of the Swedish people do not favor the EU. Three of the major parties—the Social Democrats, the Center party, and the Christian Democrats—are split on the issue. The political leadership has failed in its duty to illuminate the the national security dimensions of membership in the EU.

In Finland, on the other hand, public opinion has not played a role in foreign and security affairs in the postwar era. President Urho Kekkonen, who for many years dominated the Finnish scene, used his power to manipulate the public and probably even instigated the note crisis with the Soviet Union in 1961 to strengthen his grip over the government. National security decisions were taken by a small, close-knit elite, probably the most able group in Northern Europe. Unlike its Scandinavian neighbors, Finland is a war-fighting nation. Three times in this century it has thwarted Soviet offenses and has come through freer and more confident than ever. Thus it was not even necessary to explain the security dimension to the Finnish public when the issue of the EU came up on the agenda. Fifty-six percent of the Finnish public voted to join and, unlike in Sweden, Europe has remained consistently popular in Finland ever since.

But Finland's solid pro-European stance has not prevented a more lively debate on other issues concerning security. After the cold war that debate has separated the Social Democrats (who now are in power with both the presidency and the office of prime minister) from the old establishment party, the Center party (Kekkonen's old party, currently headed by Esko Aho). Even other parties have managed to enter the political arena. One such party provided one of the major candidates for the presidency in 1994, Elisabeth Rehn. A new libertarian party in Parliament is headed by the foreign policy expert Risto Pentillä.[9] In May 1996 the veteran diplomat Max Jacobson predicted that Finland, together with Sweden and Austria, would apply for membership in NATO after Poland, the Czech Republic, and Hungary.[10]

Norway is yet another story. Twice in one generation, in 1972 and in 1994, the establishment was defeated by the periphery on national security issues: the all-important question of joining the EU. The oil glut of the 1970s and 1980s contributed to the defeat. For two decades Oslo invested the revenue from Norway's oil and gas resources in the infrastructure of the periphery, the coast and the fjords. As a consequence, fishermen, small farmers, and public sector civil servants of western and northern Norway achieved a higher standard of living heavily subsidized by the central government. Shipping, another Norwegian tradition, filled out the picture. As an Atlantic nation tied to the Anglo-Saxons, Norway distrusted Europe, and since the natural resources provided well for Norway's citizens it decided to remain outside the EU. The sustained efforts of the Norwegian establishment to build security bridges to the European continent failed. This, of course, made Norway's NATO membership more important than ever.

Finally, Denmark had an anti-authoritarian public, just like Norway. As a small nation, suspicious of supra-European schemes, Denmark was the only nation to vote against the Maastricht Treaty at first. In NATO, Denmark has been known as the "footnote nation," putting its own stamp on decisions that in the larger nations of Europe have been uncontroversial or considered necessary. But in the end Denmark, given its geography, is boxed in, integrated into the EU and NATO both economically and militarily. Unlike the other peripheral nations of Northern Europe, Denmark has nowhere else to go. With its room to maneuver limited, it has no choice but to grin and enjoy it, as it now does with its extraordinarily close and friendly relationship with the new Germany.

The Russian Threat

The three main security threats to Europe in the post–cold war era can be categorized as eastern turmoil, southern turmoil, and southeastern (Balkan) turmoil. In the East there is Russia, a nation that will not belong to the new Western security regime. Through Finland, the EU has acquired a new 1,200 km border with Russia. As Josef Joffe, the foreign policy expert of the *Süddeutsche Zeitung* in Munich, put it, "Russia will be neither fully democratic nor pacific for a long time. Indeed, the process seems to be reversing ever so slowly. Russia is trying to reconstitute the former Soviet empire: peacefully where possible, violently when necessary. Whatever its domestic constitution Russia is simply too "big" for Europe; it remains, as in the Czarist and Bolshevik past, a problem in the European balance." [11]

"The problem with Russia in the foreseeable furture is not its strength, but its instability," to quote Christoph Bertram, the diplomatic correspondent of *Die Zeit* in Hamburg. [12] Because of this instability, upheaval, civil war, nuclear reactor failures, nuclear warheads adrift, ecological disasters, and pollution all pose potential dangers to the nations on the Baltic and Arctic Seas. [13] But even so, the old-fashioned threats to Scandinavia remain, albeit on a diminished scale for the time being. The troops in the Leningrad Military District have the most modern equipment in the Russian armed forces. Trouble in the Baltic states may lead to pressure, blackmail, or even aggression. The breach of the Conventional Armed Forces in Europe (CFE) Treaty on the northern flank in the Leningrad Military District is yet another sign of conflict. Kaliningrad, with its high concentration of Russian troops, could also cause problems. Finally, the Kola base system, which in the future may house all Russian nuclear submarines and 50 percent of the entire Russian nuclear strategic force, will remain a key area for the defense of Russia. The perimeter around the Kola complex will be secured, but how wide and secure that perimeter needs to be to satisfy a suspicious Russian regime remains to be seen. All these contingencies would stem from an as yet unseen reconstituted Russian threat, a threat that would be most serious, should it appear. Unlike for the countries of Central Europe, the military geography of Finland, in particular, has not improved after the cold war.

The U.S. Role

Maintaining a U.S. presence in Europe is of course the basis for the continued viability of NATO and the Western security regime. This has always been the working assumption of the Nordic nations, but unlike during the cold war this assumption is now also verbalized by Finland and Sweden. The problem for Europe, therefore, is to maintain the interest of the United States in European security so that NATO does not turn into a hollow shell. According to Jim Thomson of the RAND Corporation, America's interest in Europe has been downgraded from vital to important since the cold war and the disappearance of the Soviety enemy on the continent.[14] Working with the United States on NATO expansion and as a global partner is what is required of Europe, according to Thomson. Among the nations specifically singled out by Thomson are Germany and Norway—Germany because it will be the most important nation of the future Europe and Norway because of its military geography. But if Norway is singled out in this way, then certainly Sweden should be as well, since the former cannot be defended without the latter.

The task of keeping America interested in Europe is complicated by the failure of European leaders to explain the facts to their publics. With Western Europe now enjoying a sense of security, it is difficult to spell out why it is necessary for the United States to stay involved on the continent. Central and East European nations, because of their historical experience, have no such problems of comprehension; West Europeans might.

The Norwegian historian Rolf Tamnes has outlined three distinct geostrategies in American policy in Northern Europe: the continental strategy, the strategic nuclear perspective, and the maritime strategy.[15] In the continental strategy, Norway is an integral part of the defense of Europe, serving as a strategic flank to the central front. Developed in the late seventies, this strategy was a reaction to the Soviet naval buildup, which threatened Atlantic sea lanes. The strategic nuclear perspective, in the age of strategic nuclear weapons with intercontinental range, U.S. requirements for early warning and intelligence focused on the Nordic region because the most important flight paths for bombers and missiles passed through it. The possibility that the Soviets might use the region for staging operations against North America and the buildup of the Kola base complex made the region even more interesting. The maritime strategy of the Reagan years took on a forward quality. Operations were staged to put pressure on Soviet strategic submarines and to deny the Soviet Navy access to open seas. In this strategy, Northern Europe changed from being a flank to being an important area in the U.S.-Soviet arms race.

Today, the strategic nuclear perspective remains the strongest, given the importance of the Russian Kola base complex. The continental strategy has become less important since the disappearance of the threat to the European continent. The continental strategy for Norway spelled sea lines of communications (SLOCS) and SLOCS are gone when that strategy is gone. The maritime strategy would be important in a more isolationist America.

The United States remains the most important nation among the four big friends of Northern Europe—the others are the United Kingdom, Germany, and France. Unlike Russia, a potential adversary, these four nations will play vital roles in the Western web of collective security that has been spun around the European continent. How the strategic development and capabilities affects the Nordic nations will be discussed at length in chapter 2. Despite all its aspirations the EU will not be as important as NATO when it comes to the hard-core defense of the nations under study. Most international security actions in the post–cold war world are likely to fall outside the realm of Article V. (Article V of the North Atlantic Treaty provides that, in the event of an armed attack against one or more NATO members, the other members will assist the member that has been attacked.) Thus it will be easy to lose sight of NATO's original function, although that function was upheld by the guidelines concerning the organization's "strategic concept" agreed to at NATO's Rome summit in November 1991.

The Petersberg declaration, issued by the Western European Union in June 1992, sums up all the other actions to be undertaken by NATO. At the EU's Intergovernmental Conference (IGC) beginning in 1996, the United Kingdom has taken an attitude different from those of France and Germany. The United Kingdom wants to maintain the separation between the EU and the WEU. So do Sweden and Finland. (This issue will be discussed further in chapter 3.) All Nordic nations are now willing to show goodwill and contribute to non–Article V actions taken by NATO, even though this does not provide Article V protection to the non-NATO members. The reasons for this goodwill are several. Sweden wanted to get into the EU and viewed participation in NORDBAT in the former Yugoslavia as a showcase for its membership. Finland, with its track record in European security, did not need to show the flag in Bosnia and also had constitutional problems in sending troops abroad for peace-enforcing missions. Not only have Norway and Denmark assigned forces to international actions under UN or OSCE command, but the same units also have special roles in NATO's Immediate Reaction and Rapid Reaction Forces. The main contribution to European security provided by these nations is the defense of their own territory, thereby creating a stable environment in Northern Europe. The international operations in the limelight thus form only a small proportion of the real defense efforts of Sweden, Finland, Norway, and Denmark. The bottom line is simple: If NATO is the only serious institution when it comes to the defense of Europe it is a vital interest for the Nordic nations to preserve NATO, but an important, although perhaps not vital, interest for the United States in Jim Thomson's vocabulary. For the non-NATO Nordic states it is also important to keep open the option to join NATO if that in time should be necessary, to make the most of the PFP and all that comes with it, and to create close cooperation with the four key NATO members through cooperation on procurement, staff talks, standardization, and interoperability. Two questions remain however: Will all non–Article V actions be money in the bank if the Nordics ever face an Article V situation? and, Is it even likely that they would face an Article V situation alone if they are members of the EU?

Notes

[1] *Sverige i Europa och världen* (Stockholm: Försvarsdepartementet, 1995), quoted in Jan Foghelin, *Perspectives on Sweden and NATO* (Stockholm: FOA, February 1996), 11–12.

[2] Ibid.

[3] *Security in a Changing World* (Helsinki: Council of State, June 1995), 67.

[4] Thus Krister Wahlbäck's clever article, "Aderton missförstånd om svensk säkerhetspolitik," (*Internationella Studier* 3, [1995], 37–80) has the purpose of assuring the elite that all options are still open.

[5] Peter Bröms, Johan Eriksson, and Bo Svensson, *Reconstructing Survival: Evolving Perspectives on Euro-Arctic Politics* (Stockholm: Fritzes, 1994).

[6] John J. Mearsheimer, "The False Promise of International Institutions," *International Security* 19:3 (Winter 1994/95), 5–49. Like Mearsheimer, I consider myself a realist and believe that "institutions reflect state calculations of self-interest based primarily on concerns about relative power" (John J. Mearsheimer, "A Realist Reply," *International Security* 20:1 (Summer 1995), 82). That is why institutionalists in the past seldom discussed NATO.

[7] Philip Zelikow, "The Masque of Institutions," *Survival* 38:1 (Spring 1996), 7.

[8] Karl Deutsch et al., *Political Community and the North Atlantic Area: International Organization in the Light of Historical Experience* (Princeton: Princeton University Press, 1957).

[9] Risto Pentillä wants Finland to approach NATO in peacetime and develop an international defense policy and capability. See Pentillä, "Arvosidonnaisen ulkopolitiikan ansat," *Ulkopolitiikaa* 3 (1995), quoted in Arto Nokala, "Finland's Security Policy '95: Consolidation and Main Discussions," in *Yearbook of Finnish Foreign Policy 1995* (Helsinki: Finnish Institute of International Affairs, 1996).

[10] Max Jakobson, "Finland: A Nation that Dwells Alone," *Washington Quarterly* 19:4 (Autumn 1996), 55.

[11] Josef Joffe "Is There Life after Victory? What NATO Can and Cannot Do," *National Interest* 41 (Fall 1995), 25.

[12] Christoph Bertram, *Europe in the Balance* (Washington, DC: Carnegie, 1995), 33.

[13] Tomas Ries, *North Ho: The New Nordic Security Environment and the European Union's Northern Expansion* (Sankt Augustin: Konrad Adenauer Stiftung, November 1994), 29. See also Appendix.

[14] James A. Thomson, *Paper for American-German Conference*, Konrad Adenauer Stiftung, Sankt Augustin, February 7, 1995.

[15] Rolf Tamnes, *The United States and the Cold War in the High North* (Oslo: Ad Notam, 1991), 296–7.

Chapter 1

The Setting: Psychological and Institutional Restraints

Little Interest in Northern European Security

In the turmoil that has enveloped Southeastern Europe after the end of the cold war, Northern Europe has received scant attention.[1] Despite its unruly neighborhood—including northwest Russia, St. Petersburg, and the Baltic states—the North has been a relatively quiet part of Europe since 1989. During the cold war, too, this was a calm area; Finland and Sweden provided a neutral buffer zone separating the two superpower blocs in Europe. Norwegian and Danish restraint on nuclear issues and on movements of foreign troops also kept confrontation at a minimum. Finally, the iron fist of Soviet forces in the three Baltic states, in Poland, and in East Germany, kept internal turmoil at bay, at least until 1980 when the glacier was broken in Poland. This tradition of restraint continued into the post–cold war era. Baltic independence was reached with a minimum of bloodshed, and in East Germany, as in Poland, the Soviet troops left in a peaceful, orderly fashion.[2]

It is not surprising, then, that when the issue of NATO expansion was first raised, it was with regard to Central Europe, not the North. Of the former captive nations of Eastern and Central Europe it was Poland, Hungary, the Czech Republic, and, to varying extents, the Slovak Republic and Slovenia that considered themselves to be on the forefront of NATO expansion; they were regarded similarly in the West.[3] Despite occasional Swedish encouragement no one expected the Baltic states to be able to join NATO within the foreseeable future. Likewise, Romania, Bulgaria, and Albania, not to mention Belarus and Ukraine, were simply not in the cards. Because of geopolitical realities, Germany became the champion of NATO expansion in Central Europe; for reasons connected with Western leadership as well as ethnic domestic politics, the American national security elite also took a leading role in promoting the expansion issue. Since the two obvious candidates for NATO membership, Finland and Sweden, both of which fulfilled all the criteria,[4] expressed no interest, they naturally were left out of the debate.

The Sidelining of Norway

Norway, one of the founders of NATO and since 1949 one of its staunchest supporters, gradually became marginalized during the debate over NATO expansion. Since the Soviet threat in Northern Europe had receded, less attention was lavished on Norway than during the 1980s and the times of U.S. Secretary of the Navy John Lehman's maritime strategy.[5] In fact, Washington proposed the elimination of all but two of the nine co-located operating bases (COBs) allocated to the U.S. Air Force in Norway in times of crisis or war. Only after a vigorous intervention did the Norwegians manage to set the number of COBs at five rather than two. The fate of the U.S. Marine Corps mission in Tröndelag, Norway, meticulously built up during the 1980s, remains in doubt. For the time being the equipment remains in place and the mission stays in the plans.

The realignment of the NATO command structure dealt another blow to Norway. For decades the headquarters of NATO's northern command, CINCNORTH, had been located in Kolsaas, outside Oslo. In 1994, a new command was created for Allied Forces Northwestern Europe, AFNORTHWEST, that covered Norway, the United Kingdom, and adjacent waters. The new command was located in High Wycombe, outside London. CINCNORTH was dissolved. Denmark, which together with the northern German state of Schleswig-Holstein had been within the scope of CINCNORTH before realignment, now comes under the Central European Command (AFCENT) at Brunsum, the Netherlands; with this reorganization the Norwegian connection with the European continent has been broken. The navies of Norway, the United Kingdom, Denmark, and Germany are kept under dual command AFCENT or NAVNORTHWEST to be assigned to the Baltic or the North Sea depending on the situation.

But the biggest blow to Norway was the refusal of its electorate to join the EU. With Norway in the EU the coordination of policies among the four Nordic nations would have been easy. Now Finland, Sweden, and Denmark are members of the EU and Norway is not. Despite efforts to influence events informally, Norwegian decisionmakers quickly realized that there is no substitute for membership.

Within NATO, planning has proceeded as before and Norwegian concerns are given a special interest. But when Russia broke the CFE Treaty in November 1995, Washington and Moscow decided to look the other way; Norway, together with Turkey, the most stalwart supporter of orthodoxy, was overruled. Concerns about the Russian-American relationship took precedence over the legitimate worries of the nations on NATO's northern and southern flanks.

THE INCREASING IMPORTANCE OF DENMARK, SWEDEN, AND FINLAND

Denmark and Finland have gained the most from the breakup of the Soviet Union and the withdrawal of Russian troops from East Germany, Poland, the Baltic states, and Belarus. Instead of having a Soviet tank Army at its doorstep, Denmark is now fully 1,000 km east of the battered Russian forces, protected from them by not only the Bundeswehr but also the emerging Polish armed forces. The new command structure of NATO has made Denmark essentially a part of Germany, from a security standpoint. To counter German dominance in this scenario, Denmark is using the British and, to a lesser extent, the American card. The Zealand armored brigade that also serves as the Danish International Brigade, has a double role together with the British First Armored Division based in Hessen, Germany. The British-Netherlands Amphibious Force still has a role in Jutland in the war plans. But geopolitically Denmark's fate lies with that of the European continent. Recognizing this, Danish Defense Minister Hans Haekkerup has used every opportunity to cultivate ties with his German and Polish counterparts. Denmark is the only Nordic nation that has membership in both NATO and the EU, and that is exactly why its Nordic identity can be questioned.

Finland and Sweden, newcomers to European security policy, have changed the most since the end of the cold war, and that is why most of this study has to be dedicated to them. Both countries are eminently qualified to join NATO but neither of them wants to do so for the time being. In fact, Sweden has emitted mixed signals ever since it discovered that the cold war is over. Just as former German chancellor Willy Brandt thought that the disappearance of the German Democratic Republic would constitute a crushing defeat for European social democracy,[6] so did many of his Swedish party brethren, even if it was politically incorrect to say so at the time.

At the same time, the membership of Finland and Sweden in the EU and other organizations has raised Western expectations of their contribution to Northern European security to an often unrealistic level. To some extent Carl Bildt's rhetoric while he was prime minister of Sweden is responsible for these expectations; outside observers often read more into his statements on Baltic security than was prudent. Yet even in 1995, with Bildt out of power, German statements on Baltic security were overly optimistic and missed a crucial point: the Nordic nations as a regional group are unwilling and unable to solve the security problems of their three small Baltic neighbors. Only German preoccupation with Central Europe and Russia, with the Balkans, and their unwillingness to go there with America and France can explain the cavalier and hasty attention paid to Baltic security matters. Be that as it may, the German attitude toward Nordic security sometimes spread even to experienced American analysts, who got the message but overinterpreted it.[7] The Nordic nations, for their part, sometimes had problems explaining exactly what their contributions to European security would be. In this effort Sweden in the beginning was less successful than Finland.

The question remains how ready the newcomers are to participate successfully in the transatlantic security policy. The time tables of European and Western institutions rather than the time tables of internal policies, will force upon the Nordic nations important and often unwelcome decisions. Moments of truth will appear, not because they are welcome but simply because they have been put on the agenda by other, more powerful European nations.

The North Is Different

For most of the democracies of Western Europe, NATO has been the preeminent security organization since its formation in 1949. But five Western European democracies have remained outside of the NATO security architecture: Ireland, Switzerland, Sweden, Austria, and Finland. Defeat in World War II forced Austria and Finland to settle for neutrality, certainly a solution preferable to the slavery imposed upon their more unfortunate eastern neighbors. The three others, which managed to stay out of the war, continued their policy of nonalignment after Germany's defeat. Since they did not belong to NATO and until 1995 also were not members of the European Community, they relied upon the other available organizations for their security needs—namely, the United Nations (except for Switzerland) and, as it came into being, the Organization for Security and Cooperation in Europe (OSCE). Neither Finland nor Sweden had many options because, to use the Norwegian strategist Johan Jörgen Holst's words, the former was constrained by its past failures and the latter by its successes.[8]

Using the instruments of the UN skillfully for self-promotion required a whole subculture of rites and ceremonies, procedures and preliminaries. Surely diplomats and veteran journalists understood the difference between hope and reality, and were able to put the real contributions of the Nordic nations into perspective. The Nordic publics overestimated the Nordic influence at the UN. They were deceived by pomp and ceremony into thinking something was getting done; they misunderstood the power of the UN and thought it provided security for them.

With the UN ethos came assignments of mediation, diplomacy, and even prominence at times.[9] Various peacekeeping plans required forces: 70,000 troops over the years from Sweden and 30,000 from Finland. Thus the Nordic nations provided public goods to the world community and were sometimes praised for it. No wonder that the underlying structure of Western security, that is, the deterrence and defense posture of NATO, by and large was left undiscussed in the security milieu of the Northern European nations.

The beginnings of the OSCE at the Helsinki conference raised hopes and were met with enthusiasm in the North for the same reason that they were met with skepticism, and even hostility, in the United States. Here, the two blocs met in the same forum as did all the neutral parties (the latter were kept out of the other East-West meetings). The OSCE was, in a sense, the UN writ small. In June 1992 the OSCE was even proclaimed to be a regional organization of the UN, but in the areas of politics and culture, not security, as security specialist Catherine Kelleher has pointed out.[10]

Thus in the aftermath of the cold war Finland and Sweden were geared to create a *European* security regime, a Europe not creating new borders.[11] They were not used to the thought of a *Western* security regime, because they incorrectly still fancied themselves as mediators and healers of European security problems. Realism was stronger in Finland where, on the face of it, Helsinki maintained the policy originating with the Helsinki process—which implied continued Finnish dependence on Russia. A few key policy makers began dismantling this dependency on the USSR and Russia that had stifled Finnish action ever since 1944. Sweden, which for many reasons could remain much more passive, had no such need to break old habits. The name of the game in Stockholm was to slip into the EU as unobtrusively and smoothly as possible without awakening the fears of neutralist fundamentalists. Thus when the issue of NATO expansion came on the agenda of Western security discussions, Sweden made a false start, proclaiming that such measures would create new borders in Europe and violate the vision of an all-European security order. After a period when it became embarrassingly clear that only Russia shared that point of view in Europe, such declarations became scarce. Yet the notion remained and made Swedish new thinking difficult. While the Central and Eastern European nations wanted to join the West in the shortest possible time, Sweden envisioned a European security order where the distinction between East and West, in the cold war sense, was no longer important.

Thus the irony persisted that both Sweden and Finland met the criteria of NATO membership as outlined in the study on NATO enlargement of September 1995, yet, unlike the Central European states and Austria (the third new member of the EU), they were not prepared to take the step of joining. Finland, having undertaken an internal study in the fall of 1995, has concluded that NATO membership is not desired for the time being. In Sweden, nonmembership in NATO is a dogma that currently is neither studied nor challenged by national security policy insiders.

But it is not only the mind frame of Sweden and Finland that is different. Because of their neutrality, their defense efforts are exclusively national. At a time when renationalization is seen as a major problem of Western defense, the Nordic nations start out nationalized. While Norway and Denmark are integrated into NATO through their infrastructures; base systems; command, control, communications, and intelligence (C³I) systems; reinforcement plans; joint maneuvers; and nuclear postures, Finland and Sweden have nevertheless benefited from a strong NATO presence in the region. The reverse was also true for Denmark and Norway, of course, under the shadow of the powerful Swedish Air Force, and in Norway's case the Swedish Army, which protected the heartland in and around Oslo. Norway's dependence on its Anglo-Saxon allies and Denmark's dependence on Germany spell further integration into the Western security system.

How, then, can Finnish and Swedish defense be integrated into the Western security system without their actually joining NATO? It is assumed that these two nations and Austria are too small to set a bad example for the other Europeans. Since operations other than defense against direct attack (as provided for in Article V of the North Atlantic Treaty) are the largest tasks ahead, international operations will be increasingly common. The national contingencies of the Nordic states depend on each other and larger nations for logistics, airlift, communications, intelligence, and mutual support. In NORDBAT the Swedish and Danish forces have been integrated into one battalion. The Nordic forces in Bosnia are also integrated on a larger scale into the Nordic Brigade. NATO's Partnership for Peace (PFP) will provide the general framework for cooperation of a less dramatic, unobtrusive, but important nature. At the end of a five-year period, the armed forces of Scandinavia will be used to work together in the field. Through the EU, three out of the four Nordic nations will be able to coordinate their decisions on a routine basis. Through informal contacts with the Western European Union (WEU) and NATO, all these nations will grow accustomed to international teamwork. Meanwhile, the UN machinery will be kept on a back burner despite the strong UN ideology that exists in the Nordic nations.

A third characteristic that keeps the Nordic nations apart from many of their continental friends is their attitude toward nuclear weapons. Nobody has summarized the Nordic posture better than Holst.

> All of the Nordic states are technically capable of developing nuclear weapons, and with the possible exception of Iceland, all have economies that could sustain a nuclear weapon program. Yet they have all signed and ratified the nonproliferation treaty and the partial test ban treaty. None of the aligned states in Nordic Europe permit the deployment or storage of nuclear weapons on their territories, including the Atlantic islands. Nordic Europe constitutes a de facto nuclear weapon–free area. Sweden was the only country to consider an independent nuclear option seriously. Norway and Denmark considered permitting the storage of nuclear munitions for theater weapons, but the military arguments in favor of it were not very powerful and failed to overcome the broadly based social opposition to nuclear weapons. In addition, concerns with regard to regional and international order worked against the nuclear option.
>
> There is undoubtedly a certain amount of romantic escapism in the Nordic posture on nuclear weapons, a nostalgia for innocence, a wish to keep the ugly realities of potential destruction out of reach and out of mind. On the one hand, the Nordic NATO states have sought protection under the American nuclear umbrella, and Sweden and Finland have benefited from the nuclear stalemate; on the other hand, acceptance of nuclear abstinence has been transformed into an almost aggressive self-righteousness combined with a subliminal rejection of the dependence on nuclear guarantees. A rational decision in favor of the conventional option has tended to provide a basis for rectitude in relation to states where governments applied a different calculus. The absence of direct involvement in the management and operational planning for the possible use of nuclear weapons has tended to breed propensities for absolute rejection. This is not to deny the serious ethical issues raised by nuclear weapons, but only to point out that the public debate in the Nordic countries tends to ignore or reject the strategic issues involved. The Nordic societies have not been

continuously engaged in the nuclear debate, which is essentially an imported product reflecting decisions and challenges in other European countries, but which is given the imprint of Nordic innocence and sincerity. Scandinavians tend to view their own position on nuclear weapons in absolute rather than derivative terms. Their actual decisions on nuclear weapons are nevertheless based on solid and rational calculation. Norway is a front-line state, and reliance on nuclear weapons could involve reliance on breaking the tradition of non-use that has been in force since Hiroshima and Nagasaki. That seemed like more of a burden than Norwegian authorities were willing to carry. In view of Norwegian proximity to key strategic installations in the Soviet Union where nuclear and conventional, as well as strategic and theater, weapon systems and targets are intermingled the dangers of escalation and explosive preemption might cause the United States as well to renege on a commitment to early use in an actual situation. The psychological problems of commitment and reassurance among the Allies are compounded by nuclear deployments, and they could become a particular burden on a social consensus in small states. Furthermore, reliance on nuclear weapons may tend to weaken the national will for defense in smaller countries, as the task becomes wrapped in abstractions beyond calculation and prediction, and success moreover tends to elude credible definition. It is far easier to mobilize protest against nuclear weapons than to design schemes for their possible use in combat.

Nuclear deterrence may be accepted as an inescapable and even necessary temporary expedient for peace at large, but the Nordic people do not want their sons to fight with nuclear weapons. They have become used to the notion that nuclear weapons are not for use. Theater weapons carry connotations of use in a more immediate and concrete manner than strategic weapons. They have been rejected as an option by all of the Nordic states. Such rejections have tended to ferment into orthodoxy. Decisions that were controversial in the early sixties have become consensus positions in the eighties, making it harder for the aligned countries to participate in consultations and decisions about nuclear weapon deployments in the alliance. Hence, decisions that contributed toward reaching a consensus about defense in the sixties may complicate the maintenance of a consensus about alliance policy in the eighties. None of the aligned states in Nordic Europe, however, has protested against established NATO doctrine, nor has any expressed the desire to come out from under the U.S. nuclear umbrella. Furthermore, in an actual war, Nordic Europe could not escape the effects of nuclear warfare even if such weapons were not used against or from Nordic territory. The fallout from nuclear explosions in Central Europe and the Soviet Union would be carried by the winds into the Nordic world.[12]

This attitude spells dissent and conflict over the nuclear future of Europe, especially the French version. If France is to take a leading role in European security, as many now wish, the Nordic nations will be marginalized not only on the nuclear issue but on other issues as well. Even the United Kingdom pursues a policy that is not accepted by the Nordics when it comes to nuclear deterrence. Of the three European powers Germany's nuclear policy is most to the liking of the Nordic states. If renationalization prevails in Germany, or if the United States loses interest in Europe, the likely result—a German reversal in this field—will have an immediate and frightening effect on the Northern body politic.[13]

Traditional Issues: Arms Control and Kaliningrad

Cold war arms control agreements define the security environment of Northern Europe. The second Strategic Arms Reduction Treaty (START II) limits the type and number of Russian strategic nuclear weapons based at Kola and their role in the Russian strategic nuclear force. The CFE Treaty limits the number of conventional weapon systems in Norway, Denmark, Poland, and various military districts and oblasts in Russia. Any breach of these treaties can serve as a warning signal if events are moving the wrong way. Similarly, the Russian troops based in Kaliningrad, which are not limited by treaty, can also serve as an indication of Russian capabilities, if not intentions.

START II

START II was concluded between the United States and Russia in January 1993. At the time the United States deployed roughly

10,000 nuclear warheads, and Russia, Belarus, Ukraine, and Kazakstan roughly 11,000 nuclear warheads, as part of their strategic weapon systems. According to START II each side is to reduce their number of nuclear warheads to 3,500 by January 1, 2003.

The most important change occurs in Russia where heavy intercontinental ballistic missiles (ICBMs) represented 60 percent of the existing warheads in 1993. Under START II the heavy SS-18s will be eliminated, as will all ICBMs with multiple independent re-entry vehicles (MIRVs). By 2003, ICBMs will represent only 18 percent of the warheads. The possible development of the structure of the strategic forces of the two sides is shown in Table 1.1.

Since the United States has a strategic advantage at sea it will have won yet another strategic victory if the START II agreement is implemented as planned. For the Kola area the implementation is even more ominous. As Table 1.1 and 1.2 indicate, 50 percent of all Russian strategic warheads would be based in the Northern Fleet. Each submarine would carry 5 percent of the entire Russian strategic nuclear arsenal. This, of course, would make the security of each strategic submarine based at Kola extraordinarily important. The Norwegian journalist Jan Otto Johansen has even spoken of the Kola area as the 1990s equivalent of the Russian Karelian isthmus, a dispute over which prompted Stalin to launch the 1939 Winter War on Finland to seize land considered

TABLE 1.1

PERCENTAGE COMPOSITION OF STRATEGIC FORCES IN THE
UNITED STATES AND RUSSIA, 1993 AND 2003 (PROJECTED)

		1993[1]	2003[2]
Intercontinental ballistic missiles (ICBMs)	United States	24%	14%
	Russia	60	18
Submarine-launched ballistic missiles (SLBMs)	United States	36	48
	Russia	25	53
Bombers	United States	40	38
	Russia	14	29

[1]Russia, Ukraine, Belarus, and Kazakstan
[2]Russia only
SOURCE: Based on *Treaty between the United States of America and the Russian Federation on further reduction and limitation of strategic offensive arms*, Moscow, January 3, 1995; and *The Military Balance 1995–96* (London: International Institute for Strategic Studies, 1995), 15.

TABLE 1.2
PROJECTED COMPOSITION AND BASE LOCATION OF RUSSIAN STRATEGIC NAVAL FORCES, 2003

Class of submarine	Number of submarines	Total number of missiles	Total number of warheads	Percentage of total submarine forces	Percentage of total SLBM warheads
Kola					
Borey	1	12	120		
Delta 4	7	112	1,120		
Typhoon	1	20	200		
	9		1,440	75%	97%
Pacific					
Delta 3	3	48	48	25%	3%

SOURCE: Communication from Norman Polmar, January 1997.

by the Soviets to be important to the safety of Leningrad.[14] Could leaders in Moscow in the future regard the Kola complex so important to Russian security that they would consider a defensive zone around it necessary, and how large would such a zone be, given new military technologies? Might Moscow, in other words, contemplate military action against its neighbors in the North in order to safeguard its nuclear assets based at Kola? If so, what neighbors and with what targets in mind? Since all strategic submarines would be at sea when a war broke out, such a zone has to be created in advance, if at all. At present, such speculations seem morbid; a policy maker in an embattled and authoritarian future Russia may not find them as farfetched.

The ratification and implementation of the START agreements are a bilateral affair where not even the nations of the EU have an impact. It is possible that Russia during the decade ahead will find it prudent to steer more resources to its remaining land-based deterrent and that the START II agreement will not be implemented as it was originally planned.[15] Furthermore, the CFE breach may have a spillover effect on START, especially since Moscow can claim that START, like the CFE, was negotiated while Russia was in a weakened position. Even though such a re-allocation of Russian strategic resources would be in the Nordic interest, formidable resources will remain at Kola. Moscow will want to secure that region no matter what, and the strategic assurance it seeks from the West will have to be worked out between the United States and the nations bordering on that region.

THE CFE

After many years of negotiations the CFE Treaty was signed in November 1990. It was designed to eliminate the capability to wage large-scale offensive war in Central Europe by setting equal quantitative ceilings on the levels of conventional armaments held by members of NATO and the former Warsaw Pact. The armaments covered by the treaty fall into five categories: tanks, artillery pieces, armored combat vehicles (ACVs), combat aircraft, and attack helicopters.[16] At the Tashkent summit of the Commonwealth of Independent States in May 1992, the Soviet successor states divided up the Soviet military's equipment, an action that was formalized at the Helsinki summit of the Conference on Security and Cooperation in Europe (CSCE) in July 1992.

To meet the concerns of Norway, Bulgaria, and Turkey a two-part flank zone was incorporated into Article V of the CFE Treaty. According to Article V, Russia must divide approximately 10 percent of its total equipment between the Leningrad Military District and the Caucasus region.[17] In this two-part zone Russia was allowed a total of 600 main battle tanks (MBTs), 580 ACVs, and 1,280 artillery pieces, plus a significant amount of stored equipment in the Leningrad district. In 1993 Russia proposed the suspension of Article V, and in 1994 it specified that it wanted additional equipment in the zone on the order of 400 MBTs, 2,420 ACVs, and 820 artillery pieces. Altogether this would amount to 1,000 MBTs, 3,000 ACVs, and 2,000 artillery pieces to equip four mechanized divisions. Russia argued that the current CFE limits prevented it from restructuring its forces to meet the new strategic challenges, prevented it from adequately housing troops returning from Central and Eastern Europe, and prevented it from focusing on and protecting its southern borders, where its current security problems are. In November 1995 Russia had not fully complied with the CFE Treaty, nor had the flank zone issue been resolved, and it was only in the beginning of June 1996 that a three-year compromise solution was found. Under this compromise, Russia can field 1,897 MBTs, 4,397 ACVs, and 2,422 artillery pieces in the flank area until May 31, 1999, after which the level is to be lowered to 1,800 MBTs, 1,700 ACVs and 2,400 artillery pieces.

Although the CFE flank issue arose because of Russia's increased activities in the South, by definition it will touch on force levels in Northern Europe as well. Finland, Sweden, and the Baltic states have been beneficiaries of the treaty even though they, unlike Norway, Iceland and Denmark, do not subscribe to it. The treaty limited equipment (TLE) level in the Leningrad Military District had been set so low by the CFE treaty that it precluded a Russian conventional attack on Finland and Sweden. Even with the TLE stored in the St. Petersburg area, which can be used only with forty-two days' notice, the total equipment would not threaten the Nordic states. Assuming that Russia keeps one-third of its allocated flank TLE in the North, the balance would come out as shown in Table 1.3.

With the loss of the Baltic states and sea lift—the ability to transport troops and equipment by sea—in the Baltic, Russia will be able to invade Sweden only after a long military buildup, which would be noticed and counteracted. The CFE Treaty in its

Table 1.3
Projected Force Levels (Allocated Flank TLE) in
Northern Europe after May 31, 1999

	Number of MBTs	Number of ACVs	Number of artillery pieces
Russia*	600	1,233	800
Finland	252	1,283	918
Sweden	664	1,147	956
Norway	170	223	402

*Theoretically Russia could place all, not one-third, of its equipment in the North, but that would presume total calm on the southern flank and much turmoil for other reasons on the northern flank.

SOURCES: Russian figures based on the *Economist*, June 8, 1996, 32. Finnish, Swedish, and Norwegian figures based on *The Military Balance 1996–97* London: International Institute for Strategic Studies, 1996, 66, 87, 98.

present form caps Russian forces in the Leningrad Military District and thereby provides strategic warning in the event the treaty is broken or not implemented. Like Finland, Sweden has been more sanguine about the CFE breach in 1995, unlike Norway and Turkey. In the end, however, Norway and Turkey were overruled by the United States and Germany, who are willing to see a modified continuous treaty rather than the political consequences of a broken treaty. Meanwhile, the Nordic nations have resisted various schemes to count certain oblasts of the Leningrad Military District (namely, Novgorod, Pskov, Vologda) as belonging to a non-flank zone (defined under Article IV, section 2) and thereby to exempt them from the limitations on Russian forces stationed there. Should that happen, reason the Swedes, the Baltic states could be attacked by Russia out of the blue, without its violating the CFE limits in the area.[18]

Indeed, in the June 1996 compromise Pskov was exempted from the CFE limits. Thus, the number of ACVs in the Pskov oblast can be increased from 171 to 600—enough equipment for the Seventy-sixth Airborne Division and the Twenty-fifth Mechanized Brigade. Even if the Baltic states can already be attacked by forces based in Kaliningrad and the Leningrad Military District without breaking the CFE agreement, the pressure on Estonia and Latvia does increase because of the force levels now allowed in Pskov. But, more important, should Russia be determined to take such a crucial step as an invasion of the Baltics, the breaking of the treaty will be a very small consideration in the total calculus.

The CFE Treaty negotiated by the two cold war power blocs in Europe has brought with it a windfall profit to Nordic defense. If the treaty is broken or abrogated the symbolic effects are more important than the specific material effects in the North; since it is the military situation in the southern, not northern, zone that concerns Russia. The overall European security climate will be more important than the potential re-equipment of the standing Russian forces in the North.

Kaliningrad

Kaliningrad has become a national security issue only because of the end of the cold war. Its military potential was much more formidable in the 1980s, when the Eleventh Guards Army based in the area was to serve as the follow-on force for a Soviet invasion of Western Europe. The Baltijsk naval base still serves as the headquarters of the Russian Baltic Fleet, but whereas that fleet was a potent fighting force during the cold war, it now is an aging and far more modest symbol of power. It is important to point out that the Russian Baltic Fleet now has only two bases—one in Baltijsk and one in Kronstadt. Given its separation from the rest of Russia and its dependence on safe communications across Lithuania, Latvia, and Belarus, Kaliningrad is now a source of potential conflict. Difficult and at times acrimonious negotiations with Lithuania have produced free trade and transit agreements. But calls by the parliaments of the Baltic states to demilitarize Kaliningrad have been ignored by Moscow, which is now strengthening its hold over the special military district created there in 1994.[19]

By 1996 the initial buildup of forces in Kaliningrad, which had been increased by the Soviet withdrawal from Eastern Europe, had been reversed (see Table 1.4). The number of combat brigades went from fourteen to nine. At the same time, six divisions and eleven air regiments were withdrawn from the three Baltic states. The Kaliningrad forces maintained an offensive capability sufficient to conquer the Baltics in a short time. But these forces no longer possess the airlift or sealift power necessary for an offensive across the Baltic against Sweden or Denmark.

Given the favorable forward location of Kaliningrad, Moscow is likely to retain it with all its forces as the headquarters of the Baltic Fleet. In March 1996 Russia called for a corridor across Poland to link the enclave to Grodno in Belarus. Nevertheless, it

TABLE 1.4
Force Levels in Kaliningrad, 1990 and 1996

	1990	1996
Tank divisions	2	2 brigades
Motor rifle divisions	2	2
Artillery divisions	1	3 brigades
Airborne brigades	1	—
Naval infantry brigades	1	1
Coastal artillery regiments	1	1
Surface-to-air missile brigades	3	1
Tanks	802	850
Armored combat vehicles	1081	925
Artillery pieces	677	426
Attack helicopters	48	50
Combat aircraft	155	28

SOURCE: *The Military Balance 1995–96* (London: International Institute for Strategic Studies, 1995), 105; *The Military Balance 1996–97* (London: International Institute for Strategic Studies, 1996), 114.

has been difficult to convince the states across the Baltic Sea that Kaliningrad could be a major security problem or, for that matter, a place for economic investments. Neither Germany, Poland, Denmark, nor Sweden has acted more than symbolically in response to the forces in Kaliningrad. Their attention has turned elsewhere, to matters of greater urgency.

CONCLUSION

START, the CFE, and Kaliningrad are issues over which Russia's Nordic neighbors have little influence. START is, of course, primarily a bilateral, U.S.-Russian question. The Nordic nations can take measures to reassure the Russians about the safety of the Kola base complex. Concerning Kola, Norway the closest neighbor, has to achieve a maximum mix of reassurance and deterrence vis-à-vis Russia. Like its NATO allies, Norway will seek predictable stability in the North.

The CFE would seem to be the easiest element to influence since both Norway and Denmark are parties to the treaty and since Finland and Sweden can also make their voices heard unofficially in Vienna. But as Norway and, to a greater extent, Turkey have come to realize, their opinions do not weigh heavily when it comes to strategic deals between Russia and the United States. The CFE has brought a windfall profit to the Nordic states.

Yet this profit is still small compared with the Russian withdrawal from the Baltic states—the best boon of all to Danish and Swedish security.

Finally, Kaliningrad is in better shape from the Western point of view than it was in the 1980s. Since it is a marginal problem everywhere outside the Baltic region, neither the United States nor any major European power will focus on it. Due to its unattractiveness it will not attract economic investments and due to its marginal importance in Nordic security it will not attract political attention. It remains a source of tension but that tension will not lead to conflict unless far greater tension elsewhere in the area enhances the Kaliningrad problem. Russia will keep it as its forward fleet base in the Baltic and it will drain the treasury accordingly.

The Security Institutions

Of the four important security institutions, two—the UN and the OSCE—are designed to create an all-European security regime.[20] Yet these two institutions have become relatively less important in the last few years. They are treated in this chapter while the other two—the European Union and NATO—are given much attention later.

The United Nations

The United Nations has always been popular in the Nordic nations and 1987–92, when the organization seemed to be doing well, was no exception. Since Sweden and Finland are not NATO members the UN has been their only vehicle for international operations; some 70,000 Swedish and 30,000 Finnish soldiers have served with various UN missions. In Norway and Denmark the UN ideology is widespread and these nations, too, have a tradition of contributing to peacekeeping missions. Thus the secretary general's report for UN reform, *An Agenda for Peace*, got more attention in Scandinavia than in most parts of the world.[21] The Danish International Brigade (DIB) was created in 1994 partly in response to the report's call for a multinational stand by force. Under the leadership of its vigorous defense minister, Denmark is exploring this topic with like-minded nations around the world.

Like former Swedish prime minister Olof Palme when he was out of power, his successor Ingvar Carlsson also created a commission, which produced the report *Our Global Neighborhood* in 1994.[22] But the report arrived amid widespread disillusionment with the UN, and its impact seems to have been almost nil. The Clinton administration took office with high hopes for the UN but events in Somalia in 1993 quashed these hopes, and by 1995 President Clinton had realized that the UN was not a popular cause in the United States. In his speech calling for U.S. troops for Bosnia in November 1995, Clinton scrupulously avoided referring to the organization at all.[23]

Paradoxically, the UN tradition paved the way for Sweden and Finland to move closer to NATO, a process that culminated in battalions of both nations serving under NATO command as part of the Implementation Force for Bosnia (IFOR) in December 1995. In 1992 a Nordic battalion had been preemtively deployed in Macedonia. When this unit was relieved by an American battalion (under Finnish command), a second Swedish battalion with a Danish tank company, NORDBAT 2, was deployed to the Tuzla area in 1993. Two more battalions were rotated into Tuzla before NORDBAT 5 was transformed into an IFOR force around Christmas 1995. The deficiencies of the United Nations Protection Force UNPROFOR—corruption, partiality, lack of interoperability, and poor troop discipline—were not shared by the Nordic troops.[24] But the problems of troops curtailed in all their actions by their respective capitals and by the UN bureaucracy enhanced the impression of massive UN failure in Bosnia, and strengthened the demand for NATO intervention. Once again, NATO had shown that it is the only security organization that counts in Europe.

THE OSCE

In his massive if overly optimistic book on European security after the cold war, American ex-diplomat Jonathan Dean lists the functions of the OSCE:

1. The OSCE's main job is to contribute to the integration of Russia and other former Warsaw Pact countries in a democratically oriented European system.
2. The OSCE conducts political dialogue on the political, security and economic policies of member governments. This dia-

logue describes, clarifies, and on occasion criticizes government policy.
3. It carries out conflict prevention and crisis management activities.
4. It negotiates and coordinates the implementation of arms control, transparency and confidence-building measures.[25]

As the originator of the Helsinki process Finland has been one of the OSCE's staunchest supporters. Sweden, like other European neutrals, found a way to play a role in European security, as the Stockholm conference of 1986 showed. With Sweden in the chair of the OSCE in 1993 the organization tried in various ways to promote stability in Central and Eastern Europe as well as in the former members of the Commonwealth of Independent States. New institutions were established within the OSCE adding to its Office for Democratic Institutions and Human Rights in Warsaw and the Economic Forum in Prague: the Secretary General, the Permanent Committee in Vienna, the High Commissioner on National Minorities, the Forum for Security Cooperation, and the Conflict Prevention Center.[26] Of these, the high commissioner managed to ease relations between the majorities and Russians in Estonia and Latvia.

But the decline of the OSCE had already begun. In October 1990 the Charter of Paris had been endorsed by the OSCE.[27] Important politicians like Hans-Dietrich Genscher of Germany and Vaclav Havel of Czechoslovaki had supported the organization. In the euphoria after the cold war all Soviet successor states were admitted, so that the organization counted fifty-five members from Vancouver to Vladivostok. In this vast membership lay the seed of its own destruction, however: a consensus of fifty-two members was needed before the organization could move on any important issue. In other words, it could not move. Thus, despite institution-building the OSCE headed downhill after 1990. Because Genscher saw the OSCE replacing NATO in connection with German unification, Chancellor Helmut Kohl took a strong dislike to the OSCE.[28] In Washington and London the OSCE reminded people of the League of Nations.[29] The demise of the Soviet Union removed the need for an institution to keep Russia straight when it came to human rights, or so it was believed. Vaclav Havel discovered that his republic was not treated as an equal to the big powers and became disillusioned. In the crises of August 1991 in the Kremlin and summer 1991 in Yugoslavia, the reaction of the OSCE was timid and late. By monitoring the Bosnian elections of 1996, the organization proved its usefulness on the margin.

But above all a hardening Russian attitude and foreign policy strengthened the Eastern and Central European nations in their belief in the West, especially in NATO. These nations believed that the North Atlantic Cooperation Council (NACC) and the PFP would lead to NATO membership, as would membership in the expanding EU. The OSCE was increasingly seen as a complement to the important security organizations, i.e., NATO and the EU. Only in one trouble spot, Nagorno-Karabakh, was it realistically believed that sometime in the future a peacekeeping force of two to three thousand troops would be inserted. To Sweden and Finland the chairmanship of the Minsk process, which sought to resolve the conflict in Nagorno-Karabakh, was seen as an inexpensive and strategic way to gain insight into Russian thinking and keep conflicts under control, but it was also seen as following in the tradition of good international service, not as a mission of central importance to their security policies. Through the OSCE a code of behavior among civilized European nations was reaffirmed; this, of course, was good. More important, however, the OSCE was the one institution where Russia could be dealt with in a non-adversarial way, where other nations could keep their fingers on the Russian pulse and still give Moscow the prestige in European affairs that it craved. Until NATO expands and another institution is found for NATO-Russian relations, the OSCE will have to play this important role.

Notes

[1]In former U.S. Secretary of State James Baker's memoirs Scandinavia gets ten lines. James A. Baker III, *The Politics of Diplomacy* (New York: Putnam, 1995).

[2]Claus J. Duisberg, "Der Abzug der russischen Truppen aus Deutschland," *Europa-Archiv* 49:16 (1994), 461–9.

[3]United States Information Agency, *The New European Security Architecture* (Washington, DC: USIA Office of Research and Media Reaction, September 1995), 9, 15.

[4]Democratic government, harmonious relations with neighbor states, absence of minority problems, and viable democratically controlled armed forces. *Study on NATO Enlargement*. Brussels: NATO September 1995.

[5]Norman Friedman, *The US Maritime Strategy* (London: Jane's, 1988); John F. Lehman, Jr., *Command of the Seas* (New York: Scribners, 1988).

[6]Philip Zelikow and Condoleezza Rice, *Germany Unified and Europe Transformed* (Cambridge, MA: Harvard University Press, 1995), 90.

[7]"In Nordic Europe, the end of the cold war has left Sweden feeling so militarily threatened that it has officially stepped away from its traditional neutrality and is providing military training to officers from the Baltic states. This extraordinary but little noticed move by former prime minister Carl Bildt reverses Sweden's cynical interwar strategy of abandoning the Baltic states, discouraging Finnish assistance to them, appeasing Moscow, and supporting Finland as a buffer. Today Finland and Norway share Sweden's insecurity. We should expect Sweden and Finland in the not distant future— after their entry into the European Union—to sound out NATO for admission. The 'northern flank' countries of cold war times see NATO as more important today than in the past." William B. Odom, "Establish a Concert of Great Powers," *Orbis* 38 (Spring 1995), 162.

[8]Johan Jörgen Holst, "The Pattern of Nordic Security," *Daedalus* 113:2 (Spring 1984), 200.

[9]This explains the Swedish effort to become a member of the United Nations Security Council in 1997.

[10]Catherine McArdle Kelleher, *The Future of European Security* (Washington, DC: Brookings, 1995), 52.

[11]See, for example, the transcript of Prime Minister Ingvar Carlsson's speech to Paasikivisamfundet in Helsinki, December 14, 1994: *Utrikesfrågor 1994* (Stockholm: Ministry for Foreign Affairs, 1995), 86–7.

[12]Holst, "The Pattern of Nordic Security," 209–11.

[13]"The ultimate implication of a Western Europe minus the United States, therefore, is a nuclear-armed Federal Republic, with other West European countries to follow" (Josef Joffe, "Europe's American Pacifier," *Foreign Policy* 54 [Spring 1984], 78–9). David Calleo raised as early as 1987 the issue of German nuclear weapons. See Calleo, *Beyond American Hegemony* (New York: Twentieth Century Fund, 1987). 170–1. I did it first in Sweden in my inaugural lecture to the Swedish Academy of Military Sciences, December 8, 1987. See Ingemar Dörfer, "Kärnvapen, Europa och Sveriges säkerhet," *Kungliga Krigsvetenskapsakademiens Handlingar och Tidskrift* 3 (1988), 217–26.

[14]Jan Otto Johansen, *Norden—hva nå?* (Oslo: Atlanterhavskomitéen, 1995), and Wilhelm Agrell, *Alliansfri—tills vidare* (Stockholm: Natur och kultur, 1994), Chap. 5.

[15]John W. R. Lepingwell, "START II and the Politics of Arms Control in Russia," *International Security* 20:2 (Fall 1995), 63–91; Christoph Bluth, "Russian Attitudes to START II" *Jane's Intelligence Review* 8:3 (March 1996), 335–6.

[16]Richard A. Falkenrath, *Shaping Europe's Military Order: The Origins and Consequences of the CFE Treaty* (Cambridge, MA: MIT Press, 1995).

[17]Richard A. Falkenrath, "The CFE Flank Dispute," *International Security* 19:4 (Spring 1995), 129.

[18]Marco Smedberg, Robert Dalsjö, Hans Zettermark, *The Effect of CFE Capabilities to Wage War in the North* (Stockholm: FOA Reprint, September 1995).

[19]Ingmar Oldberg, "Kaliningrad-områdets framtid: Kasern, handelsplats eller stridsäpple?" *Internasjonal Politikk* 53:3 (1995), 335–6.

[20]An excellent discussion of all the four institutions can be found in Chapter 5, "Institutiornene" in *Dansk og europaeisk sikkerhed* (Copenhagen: SNU, 1995).

[21]Boutros Boutros-Ghali, *An Agenda for Peace* (New York: United Nations, 1992).

[22]Ingvar Carlsson and Shridath Ramphal, *Our Global Neighbourhood* (Oxford: Oxford University Press, 1995). Ingvar Carlsson presented the ideas of the report to a wider audience in "The UN at 50: A Time for Reform," *Foreign Policy* 100 (Fall 1995), 3–18.

[23]The best analysis of the UN-NATO relationship appeared while it was still thought that NATO could be a subcontractor to the UN: Patricia Chilton, Ostfried Nassauer, Dan Flesch, and Jamies Patten, *NATO Peacekeeping and the United Nations* (Berlin: British-American Security Information Council, September 1994).

[24]Charles King, "A World Waits for Signals from Bosnia," *The World Today*, 52:2 (February 1996), 32–6.

[25]Jonathan Dean, *Ending Europe's Wars* (New York: Twentieth Century Fund, 1994), 205. Until 1994 the OSCE was known as the Conference on Security and Cooperation in Europe (CSCE).

[26]Margaretha af Ugglas, "Sweden's Security Policy in Post–Cold War Europe," *NATO Review* 2 (April 1994), 10–15; Wilhelm Höynck, "CSCE Works to Develop Its Conflict Prevention Potential," *NATO Review* 2 (April 1994), 16–22.

[27]Samuel F. Wells, Jr., ed., *The Helsinki Process and the Future of Europe* (Washington, DC: Woodrow Wilson Center Press, 1990), is an example of the optimism that greeted the organization at the end of the cold war.

[28]Philip Zelikow and Condoleezza Rice, *Germany Unified and Europe Transformed* (Cambridge, MA: Harvard University Press, 1995), 175.

[29]Catherine McArdle Kelleher, *The Future of European Security* (Washington, DC: Brookings, 1995), 49.

Chapter 2

The Security Resources of the North

The Nordic Forces

Since two of the Nordic nations are not members of NATO and since the two that are members belong to different NATO commands, the force structures, present and planned, of the four Nordic nations are not coordinated or harmonized. Indeed, the Nordic community is not the most important consideration for these nations when it comes to national security: Denmark looks to Germany, Norway to the United States (and Britain), Finland watches Russia, and Sweden divides its attention among all of these nations but watches Russia the most.

In the Nordic nations the force structures are a result of the mobilization plans.[1] Incremental budgeting, bureaucratic routines, history, and inertia make them move slowly, but inexorably. In general, current force structures were conceived and introduced over a period of thirty years or more, beginning in the 1960s, almost at the time of the Cuban missile and Berlin crises. Thus the defense forces of the Nordic states do not form a tabula rasa. But gradually and sometimes quite fast, new elements have been introduced, such as the F-18 Hornet fighters in Finland or the Leopard tanks into Sweden. New forces and new concepts of deployment have been invented. But most important, new alliances have been formed and joint operations have been carried out. Such joint operations are the largest incentive to change.

What unites the Nordic forces and, indeed, justifies them to their taxpayers is the residual Russian threat. In Finland, of course, that threat is a reality, since Finland has a 1,300 km border with Russia—the only border between Russia and the EU. Norway, too, shares a border with significant Russian forces in the Kola region. Although their task is to secure the Kola base complex, their capability is considerable. In Sweden the risk of a Russian invasion across the Baltic is gone for the time being. Sweden's new defense five-year plan reflects this fact; it elaborates several scenarios that rely on strategic warning of a reconstitution of the Russian armed forces. Finally, Denmark has gained the most in its national security posture. Since the Danish armed forces were already semiprofessional and more continental, even during the cold war, the Danish force structure has not changed much. It is even more embedded in the European structure than its neighbors.

NORWAY

Of the four Nordic nations, Norway has had the greatest difficulty adjusting to the post–cold war era. Its privileged position as the star ally of the United States in NATO and its central position as the pivotal state of Nordic security in the 1980s[2] might in some quarters have led to rigidity. When the cold war ended, the Norwegian national security elite lost several political battles against foreign and domestic adversaries. The greatest defeat by far was the inability to follow Finland and Sweden into the EU in the fall of 1994.

Ever since joining NATO the Norwegian strategy has been to defend its territory until help arrives. Unlike in Denmark, in Norway the Russian threat remained unchanged after 1990, even as Russia's Northern Fleet rusted at the piers and gradually lost its offensive capability. The Norweigian infrastructure for receiving allied help, built up over the decades, remained in place and constituted one major asset in the NATO real-estate holdings. However, the three major forces that are expected to come to the aid of Norway in time of danger have shifted their tasks both when it comes to *how* Norway is to be helped—and more dangerously for Norway—to *if* Norway is to be helped.[3]

Of the NATO composite force designated for Norway only one U.S. and one German artillery battalion remain to reinforce Norwegian brigades stationed in the North. Of the Allied Command

Europe Mobile Force (AMF) six battalions from Canada, the United Kingdom, Italy, Germany, and Luxembourg can be deployed to Norway. Only five out of nine COBs remain to receive American and other allied combat aircraft. Eight U.S. squadrons, two British squadrons, and one Dutch squadron could have the Norwegian COBs as their primary destination in a European war.

The most important reinforcement of all—the Second U.S. Marine Expeditionary Force, headed for Tröndelag—is no longer a sure thing. Norway is now only one of several deployment areas for this force. The precursor of this force is the Norway Airlanded Marine Ground Task Force (NAL MAGTF), with eighty combat aircraft and seventy attack helicopters. It can reach Trondheim in four to six days, but if the Marine Corps decides that Norway is not where the action is, NAL MAGTF will not go at all. In a crisis elsewhere it is even possible that the Marines will take the equipment stored in Norway, use it at the scene of fighting, and not replace it afterward.

The U.K./Netherlands Amphibious Force has the Atlantic Islands Command as its deployment area, and Norway could be one place for a deployment. The Third Royal Marines Commando Brigade, with forty helicopters, could reach Norway in eight days. A new British helicopter carrier and a Dutch landing platform will be commissioned in 1997–98 to enhance the capability of amphibious force. At stake is not the ability of the amphibious force, but its mission in the future.

Meanwhile, the Norwegian conventional forces, in particular the Army, have gone though drastic changes.[4] Like the Swedish Army, the Norwegian Army was in 1987 hampered by old equipment. Thus the 13 brigades and 35 independent battalions that existed in 1987 will be reduced to 6 brigades and 20 battalions by 2000. Gone is the threat to southern and western Norway, where only 2 brigades and 10 battalions remain. Although NATO allies for the first time have begun to conduct exercises in Finnmark, this is due to the Open Skies arms control agreement and not to a newfound desire to defend this area conventionally.

As before, the main task of the Norwegian Army will be to hold the Tromsö area until help arrives from the NATO allies. Since only three divisions can advance effectively in the difficult terrain, Norway has assigned one division to the defense.[5] The old Sixth Division is now called Division 2000 and will comprise four brigades. The modernization of the Norwegian Navy and Air Force has proceeded simultaneously and for the same purpose—to secure the area for a limited time period. Within NATO, then, Norway promotes the same defense concept as it did before the cold war ended—maintaining that Brussels should not forget the Russian threat in the North. But several factors make the Norwegian plea less effective than before.

The first factor is Norway's failure to join the EU. Efforts to counter the negative effects of this decision, such as becoming an associate member of the WEU, cannot make up for the lack of information and influence within the EU. Norway is simply not in the loop when it comes to EU affairs, and its traditional strong standing in NATO has been undercut accordingly.

Second, the new NATO command structure has marginalized Norway.[6] In 1994 the responsibility for NATO's northern flank was transferred from CINCNORTH at Kolsaas, Norway; to Allied Forces Northwestern Europe (AFNORTHWEST) at High Wycombe, north of London. Thus the forces in Norway will be led from Britain in wartime, and Norway has to make do with the Principal Subordinate Command (PSC) North in Stavanger, which will command the forces in Norway and adjacent seas. The air and naval forces of Norway, Britain, and the North Sea will be led from High Wycombe and Nortwood in Britain. Even more than during earlier decades, Norway will be Britain's younger sibling in the staff and command structure, especially as the American, German, Dutch, and Danish presences at PSC North will be weakened.[7]

Since all of Denmark and Schleswig-Holstein now come under Allied Forces Central Europe (AFCENT) at Brunssum, the Netherlands, the Norwegian link to the continent through the old CINCNORTH is no longer there. The somewhat artificial method of putting the naval forces of Norway, Britain, Germany, Denmark, the Netherlands, and Belgium under the command of Naval Forces Northwestern Europe (NAVNORTHWEST) in Northwood, outside London, does not contstitute a meaningful link in peacetime. Through this new command structure, Norway's role as an Atlantic rather than a European power is underscored even more, and this unfortunately distances it from the EU members Denmark, Sweden, and Finland.

In addition, the creation of a new NATO command at Bielefeld, Germany, in 1992, moving to Rheindalen in 1994, Allied Command Europe Rapid Reaction Corps (ARRC), left Norway behind.[8] Like France but unlike Denmark, Norway contributes no forces to this ten-division rapid reaction force that will do the primary NATO fighting in the future. Although the United Kingdom was successful in getting the commanding post in the ARRC and contributes two divisions to the force, Norway for once was unable to use its excellent British contacts to participate. Norway's contribution to NATO is instead one frigate and one minesweeper, one F-16 squadron (no. 338) at Örland, and one infantry battalion (Telemark) earmarked for the Immediate Reaction Force of NATO.[9] The purpose of this force is to arrive early on the spot to show resolve, but rarely to fight. The real military-political action in NATO, where doctrine and equipment are tested and harmonized, will be in the ARRC, and there Norway will not be present.

Even the new concepts launched at the NATO 1994 summit—the PFP and the Combined Joint Task Forces (CJTFs)—have met only lukewarm Norwegian response. Critics maintain that the Norwegian military has been inflexible, holding on to old threat scenarios and missing opportunities for military cooperation in the evolving NATO. Skeptics are not so sure that peace has broken out in Europe.[10] Traditionalists maintain that Norway should participate in international operations only when it is directly important to Norwegian security, and that the meager new resources allocated to Norwegian defense should be devoted to the territorial defense of the nation.[11] It comes as no surprise that Norway is a traditionalist when it comes to NATO expansion and prefers NATO as it is, lest the U.S. commitment and guarantee to its European allies weaken and Norway be further sidelined.

Denmark

During the cold war Denmark belonged to CINCNORTH and was on the receiving end of allied reinforcements: the AMF, the U.K. Mobile Force, and the U.S. Marine Corps. Of all the Nordic nations, Denmark's military geography has improved the most since 1990.[12] There are no Russian troops in East Germany, Poland, and the Baltic states. East Germany is in NATO and Poland is pro-Western. The threat to the Baltic states has disappeared for the foreseeable future. Denmark has moved even closer to Gemany and now belongs to AFCENT at Brunssum. Denmark and Schleswig-Holstein are under the subcommand of Allied Forces Baltic Approaches (BALTAP) at Karup, as before, commanded by a Danish flag officer. The former Jutland division will be transformed into a Danish division with two Jutland brigades and one Zealand brigade. This division will fight together with the powerful German Sixth Panzargrenadierdivision, with 400 Leopard MBTs and 50 helicopters. The other Zealand brigade (the second) is the new DIB, specifically created in 1994 for three different tasks.[13] It is available for peacekeeping or humanitarian operations under the auspices of the UN or the OSCE, it can be assigned to NATO's ARRC, or it can be used for the territorial defense of Zealand. When assigned to the ARRC the DIB is affiliated with the U.K. First Armored Division, an arrangement that allows Denmark to participate in the ARRC, where the doctrine of NATO's warfighting forces is shaped. At the same time, this affiliation with the British forms a counterweight to the close cooperation with Germany that Danish defense increasingly practices. To give the Second Zealand Brigade international tasks also protects it from budget cuts in a nation that has seen the Soviet threat evaporate over a couple of years. In addition, Denmark has one mechanized infantry brigade, leaving it with five army brigades altogether. Given the small size of its army, Denmark gets much good publicity for its security policy.

SWEDEN

The Russian withdrawal from Central Europe and the Baltic states vastly improved the security position of Sweden, too. With the breakdown of the Russian armed forces it is estimated that a reconstituted Russian military threat will take five to ten years to emerge. Yet in 1992 the Swedish defense budget, which had been stagnant for twenty years, was actually increased. A strategic surprise attack at the vital functions of the government and the armed forces was the new scenario that justified the increased spending.[14] Despite the misearable condition of the Russian armed forces, especially in training and morale, a large amount of modern equipment remains and could be used by a reconstituted force.

A new defense plan formulated by the Social Democrats in late 1995 called for a 10 percent cut in the defense budget. This new plan distinguished between a threat that could result from the Russian Army being brought back to fighting condition and a long-range threat from a fully reconstituted and re-armed Russia. Whereas the first threat could emerge over a period of a couple of years, the longer-range threat was seen as developing over a decade. The intelligence function of the defense effort thus became more important than before. These defense decisions had a large impact on the mobilized force structure of Sweden (see Table 2.1). The armed forces of 2000 will be two-thirds the size of what the commander in chief had proposed in 1988 before the cold war ended.[15] Even so, only six of the thirteen brigades in 2000 will be able to be brought up to fighting condition in one year.[16] The others will need a longer time for reconstitution.

Because of the general conscription system a very large mobilization Army has been sustained in Sweden for a long time. But the Army was deficient both in training and equipment and would not have done well in a modern war (which fortunately never occurred). In the early 1990s the Army was therefore re-equipped with modern and surplus materiel, mostly from Germany: 120 improved Leopard 2 and 160 used Leopard 2 battle tanks, 600 CV-90s, 800 MT-LBs, and 350 BMP-1 infantry fighting vehicles.[17] The Air Force, meanwhile, was preparing for the introduction of the Swedish JAS 39 Gripen project, 140 aircraft to be delivered through 2002 and probably 60 more to follow, for a twelve-squadron all-JAS Air Force in the future.[18]

This defense effort was large enough to sustain international operations. While in opposition, the Social Democrats spoke of creating an international brigade, as in Denmark, to be assigned to peacekeeping missions. Economic realities made this target too ambitious; the current task is to create an international force to participate in operations mandated by the UN or the OSCE. Between eight hundred and fourteen hundred persons will be available to be assigned abroad at any one time.

Over time, Sweden has contributed 70,000 soldiers to UN peacekeeping missions. In 1992 a batallion was sent to Macedonia, and later, Swedish battalions joined UNPROFOR in Bosnia.

TABLE 2.1
STRUCTURE OF SWEDISH ARMED FORCES, 1987–2000 (PROJECTED)

	1987	1992	1996	2000
Army brigades	27	21	16	13
Surface ships	40	40	30	24
Submarines	12	12	12	7–9
Air Force squadrons	19	18	14	13

SOURCE: *Programplan för det militära Försvarets utveckling 1997–2001* (Stockholm: Military Headquarters, March 4, 1996), 35, 40, 41, 64; and *The Military Balance* (London: International Institute for Strategic Studies, various years).

By 1995, when five battalions had been recruited and rotated in and out of the region, NORDBAT 5 joined IFOR as part of a Nordic brigade.

As the peacekeeping and peace-enforcing missions assumed an increasingly Western and European nature, the old advantages of the Swedish defense profile turned into disadvantages. Equipment and command, control, and communications (C^3) were not compatible with NATO standards. Air power could not be deployed for the same reason. Because Sweden since 1985 no longer had any destroyers or frigates it could not participate in the naval forces sent to guard the former Yugoslavia. Denmark and Norway, on the other hand, had retained frigates and could do just that. For the time being the Swedish effort has focused on Army units.

FINLAND

While its Nordic neighbors disarmed in the 1980s and 1990s, Finland armed. By 1996 it had developed the largest and best equipped army among the Nordic states, a modern Navy, and an Air Force that soon will consist of 64 F-18C Hornets, the most potent combat aircraft in the region.[19] After mobilization the Army will have 27 brigades—10 modern Jaeger brigades, 14 infantry brigades with somewhat older equipment, 2 armored brigades, and 1 coastal defense brigade. This is a larger force than the three other Scandinavian armies put together (Norway has 6 brigades, Sweden 13, and Denmark 5, for a total of 24 brigades).

With this solid foundation in the national defense effort Finland has been able to act forcefully on the diplomatic front to remove the cold war restrictions on Finnish freedom of maneuver. Since 1990 it has been free to acquire whatever weapon system it wants, nuclear weapons excluded.

Since 1956 more than 30,000 men have served in Finland's peacekeeing missions with the UN. Not being a NATO member, Finland has no rapid reaction forces for international missions but now plans to form a rapid reaction brigade out of which one battalion at a time could be out of the country in international operations. The first battalion will be in service by 1998 (training began in the summer of 1996). This battalion will also perform traditional peacekeeping missions. Over the years the personnel trained for these missions will be placed in one Jaeger brigade that is part of the regular force structure.[20] Like the DIB, which is the rapid reaction brigade for the defense of Zealand, this Jaeger brigade would be the best equipped and on the highest alert for the defense of Finland. Altogether 2,000 troops will be available for international operations at any one time.

INTERNATIONAL FORCES

All four Nordic nations have now earmarked forces for international operations. These forces are detailed in Table 2.2. The Nordic brigade in the U.S. First Armored Division in Bosnia is the first such joint Nordic unit under NATO command. The first brigade commander is a Danish general with a Swedish brigadier as chief of staff. C^3 with division headquarters is NATO-compatible. This brigade therefore, is an important test case for a potential Nordic brigade in the future. Whether such a brigade can be integrated with a CJTF is an interesting question.

TABLE 2.2
STRUCTURE OF INTERNATIONAL FORCES
FROM THE NORDIC NATIONS

	Standing Armed Forces	International Forces		Airlift
Norway	30,000	2,000	1 battalion 1 F-16 squadron 1 frigate 1 minesweeper	6 C-130 Hercules
Denmark	33,000	4,600	1 brigade 1 F-16 squdron 1 Hawk battery 2 corvettes 2 submarines 10 patrol boats 2 minesweepers	3 C-130 Hercules
Sweden	64,000	1,400	1 battalion	8 C-130 Hercules
Finland	31,000	2,000	1 brigade	3 F-27 Fokker
Total	158,000	10,000		20

SOURCE: *Economist*, February 10, 1986.

The Western Friends

The three key nations providing additional security to the North are the United States, the United Kingdom, and Germany. France, recently touted as the linchpin of future European defense, matters much less in the North and has a different temperament than the northern states, as its recent snubs of Sweden and Denmark show. The irate French temper flashed over the Nordic reaction to French nuclear tests, but since the French bomb could play a role in the future European defense structure, its tests are far from irrelevant. Simply put, the French commitment to the northern flank has very low credibility in the North itself.

Within NATO, other nations do have planned roles in the North, notably Canada and the Netherlands. No sooner was the Canadian Air Sea Transportable (CAST) brigade in place than it was withdrawn. The current Canadian commitment consists of one infantry brigade in either the AMF or the composite force for Norway—not very impressive but in line with Canada's diminished commitment to European secuirty. The Netherlands supplies one third of the U.K.-Netherlands amphibious landing force, and also has committed several Air Force squadrons to Norway. Other NATO nations occasionally participate in naval maneuvers and standing naval forces.

THE UNITED KINGDOM

British security ties with the North go back hundreds of years, but more recently they can be traced to 1940 and the German invasion of Norway. The ill-fated Norwegian campaign that brought Winston Churchill to power also brought the Norwegian king and cabinet to London, from which the war against the German Reich was conducted relentlessly. Denmark, occupied, watched the last weeks of the war as a cliffhanger, as the armies of Montgomery and Rokossovsky raced toward Jutland. Both northern Norway and Bornholm were occupied by Soviet troops before they withdrew peacefully.

Finland and the United Kingdom ended up on opposite sides as Finland set out to continue its war against the Soviet Union in 1941. Although a condition of war existed between the two nations, hostilities never materialized. As for Sweden, Churchill throughout the war maintained a critical attitude toward its policy of neutrality, which he considered far too friendly to Germany. Thus Denmark and Norway emerged from the war grateful to London for their liberation and deeply skeptical of, if not hostile toward, the Swedish record.

This animosity, combined with geopolitical realities and American and British diplomacy, explains why the 1948–9 negotiations to create a Scandinavian Defense Union failed. When Norway decided to cast its lot with the big Western democracies, Denmark had no choice but to follow, and this froze the security situation in Northen Europe for the next forty years. Thus a British general or admiral always commanded the northern flank of NATO, based at Kolsaas outside Oslo until 1994, when the command was moved to High Wycombe, north of London, in the new AFNORTHWEST command.

Since the British commitment to the North remains the largest European effort, and since Norway is more Atlantic than European in its orientation, the United Kingdom is bound to play an important role in Nordic security even as its security role lessens in Europe.[21] After the war this was true for Sweden and Finland as well. Up until 1960 the United Kingdom was the primary provider of military technology to Sweden.[22] The Swedish Air Force was modeled on the Royal Air Force, and had a similar mission and strategy. Three generations of Swedish combat aircraft (Tunnan, Lansen, and Draken) carried British engines, and it was only with the advent of Viggen that Sweden turned to the United States for advanced military technology.[23] The Centurion tank was acquired at the same time. After a thirty-five-year period of reduced British influence in military technology, Saab in 1995 turned to British Aerospace for the marketing of the JAS Gripen outside Europe and for technical support in further developing the weapon system. When Sweden after a forty-year pause decided to restart staff talks with Western military powers in 1994, it began with the United Kingdom. Two years later those talks were being held with eleven countries, including Russia.[24] Finland also developed friendly ties with the United Kingdom and in the 1980s bought the Hawk trainer an advanced trainer to be used as a de facto combat aircraft.[25]

Peacekeeping is another important field where the Nordic nations and the United Kingdom cooperate, notably in the former Yugoslavia. Since peacekeeping is a growth field, this cooperation will be intensified. In the Baltic field the United Kingdom, with the encourgement of Sweden, has taken the lead in forming a Baltic battalion. Altogether the United Kingdom has concentrated a high proportion of its diminishing resources on the North Sea, and thereby to the Nordic area.

GERMANY

Germany, traditionally one of the great powers of the region, was for a long time hampered by its World War II history and its defeat in that war.[26] Since unification, Germany has risen again in the North. The move of the capital from Bonn to Berlin will strengthen northern Germany as it will Northern Europe; the eastern Baltic coast of Germany will again flourish, since the neighborhood of the most important city in Europe cannot remain a backwater. The three new members of the EU—Austria, Finland, and Sweden—are all "German" in their orientations, strengthening this bloc of Europe at the expense of the French and the other Mediterranean countries. Yet precisely because of the war experience, its constitutional complications, and its style in international politics, Germany's military-political activities have remained remarkably subdued.

Among the Nordic nations, Germany's closest ties are with Denmark. This relationship goes back to the joint NATO command in the Allied Land Forces Jutland (LANDJUT) organization and the inclusion of LANDJUT in the new Allied Land Forces Central Europe (LANDCENT). So close are the ties that Denmark, for all practical purposes, is now part of Germany when it comes to defense issues. To balance this relationship with Germany, Denmark has insisted that Britain have a role with assigned ground and air forces in case of crisis or war. But the Danish territory, with the exception of Greenland, is always commanded by a Danish-German team. The Danish International Brigade, however, in its role as the rapid reaction force within NATO, will team up with the British First Armored Division of the British Army of the Rhine (BAOR).

Norway was for a long time *terra non grata* to German armed forces, but beginning in the 1970s German officers were assigned to Kolsaas and now the German Navy and Army both have roles in Norway in wartime.[27] Finland (the old ally) and Sweden kept Germany at arm's length for a long time. Finland, especially, bowing to Soviet demands, had to treat the two Germanies as equals during the cold war and this sent a chill over her relations with West Germany. After the cold war Finland managed to acquire a great deal of East German equipment at low cost. Sweden did the same, also buying Leopard tanks for a long-overdue re-equipment of its armored brigades. The German military-political influence has been limited in the North, compared to its influence in the rest of Europe, but it will come into its own in the late 1990s. In the field of defense procurement, much cooperation can be foreseen. Cooperation between Saab and Dasa in producing combat aircraft seems likely for the next generation, even if the British Aerospace connection pulls Sweden into a transatlantic conglomerate.

THE UNITED STATES

The influence and power of the United States in the Nordic region widely surpasses that of Germany and the United Kingdom, even if U.S. interests are global and far more focused on other parts of the world. The inclusion of Norway and Denmark in NATO immediately brought these two nations into the global network of treaties encircling the Soviet Union. As NATO strategy on the continent evolved, the need to protect SLOCs increased the focus on real estate in the North. Without SLOCs across the Atlantic, the American defense of Europe cannot be sustained, and if Norway were lost (and Iceland), so too would be the SLOCs. In the 1980s John Lehman's Maritime Strategy added a strategic twist to the Norwegian Sea and its potential use in wartime. Through skillful Norwegian maneuvering, Oslo managed to bypass London in the NATO chain of command to deal directly ith Washington.[28] As a result the Norwegian-American security relationship contains a whole range of treaties, arrangements, plans, infrastructure, and forces that can be put in place should the need arise.

Another reason why the Nordic region is important to American strategy is the complex of nuclear strategic forces concentrated on the Kola peninsula in Russia, in particular the ballistic submarines mentioned earlier, but also "hunter-killer" submarines designed to chase American strategic submarines. With START II and the withdrawal of Ukraine, Belarus, and Kazakhstan from the USSR, the Russian strategic force is more sea-oriented than it once was. Futhermore, the largest concentration of nuclear weapons in all of Russia is now in the Kola region. Hence the Russian defense zone protecting these nuclear assets remains exceedingly important; the air defense forces protecting the Russian intellectual and industrial heartland of St. Petersburg and Moscow only magnify the importance of this region. American interests in the North are thus strategic rather than regional. During the cold war, these interests were focused on the defense of the European continent, but now, as the Russian conventional threat recedes, monitoring the nuclear weapons in the area is at the forefront of American concerns.

Because of NATO, the American presence has been greatest in Norway, Denmark, and Iceland. But Sweden, as a tacit ally, has also been a subject of American interest. In particular, the Swedish Air Force has been supported and equipped by, and indeed dependent on, the U.S. Air Force and Navy since the 1960s.[29] Many other weapon systems have been acquired from the United States. While the formal diplomatic relations between the two nations were acrimonious for a long time, especially during the Vietnam War, their military relations remained solid.[30]

In Finland's case the American connection came late and has accelerated as a result of the cold war's end. The United States never declared war on Finland during World War II, and Finland remained a popular and heroic friend of America in the cold war era, occasional musings of Finlandization notwithstanding. The symbol of Finnish-American military and political relations is the purchase by Finland of sixty-four F-18 Hornet combat aircraft, the most modern and potent combat aircraft in Scandinavia. With the Hornet, of course, comes equipment, armaments, advanced medium-range air-to-air missiles (AMRAAM), and all the other things that follow a big weapon system. The PFP, staff talks, military and political talks, and frequent visits flourish since Finland now has asserted itself as a Western power, a full-scale and important member of the EU. Through the PFP Finland is prepared to quickly acquire membership in NATO should the need arise. More than in Sweden, which until recently has been unwilling to think in new terms, the Finnish security elite is fully prepared to work together with the West.

From the PFP to IFOR

THE PFP

After the Copenhagen EU pledge of June 1993—that the six East Central European nations could join the EU if they met the political and economic criteria for membership—many Central and Eastern European nations wanted increased reassurance from the West. In short, they wanted to join NATO. Following initial signals from Russian President Boris Yeltsin in August that Russia would not oppose such developments, however, the Russian stance hardened and has remained strongly opposed to NATO expansion ever since. The PFP offer was first introduced by U.S. Secretary of Defense Les Aspin in a meeting of NATO defense ministers in Travemünde, Germany, in October 1993. When the PFP program was approved at the NATO summit in January 1994, it was viewed with suspicion by many who found it to be a stopgap measure to appease those nations that wanted full membership in NATO—a membership directed toward a resurgent Russian threat in the future.

The essence of the PFP was to create bilateral agreements between NATO and candidate members outlining particular areas and levels of defense cooperation for a clearly defined period of time. These agreements included regular military representation in a joint planning and coordination cell located at Mons, Belgium, near Supreme Headquarters Allied Powers Europe (SHAPE). In 1997, twenty-eight nations, including the Russian Federation, had signed the PFP agreement.

The PFP had five objectives:[31]
- to facilitate transparency in national defence planning and budgeting processes;
- to ensure democratic control of defence forces;
- to maintain the capability and readiness to contribute, subject to constitutional considerations, to operations under the authority of the UN and/or responsibility of the Conference (now Organisation) on Security and Cooperation in Europe (OSCE);
- to develop cooperative military relations with NATO, for the purpose of joint planning, training, and exercises in order to strengthen their ability to undertake missions in the fields of peacekeeping, search and rescue, humanitarian operations, and others;
- to develop, over the longer term, forces that are better able to operate with those of the members of the North Atlantic Alliance.

The three Baltic states joined the PFP for the same reasons that the other East and Central European nations joined. They see the PFP as an avenue to NATO membership and have done their best to integrate themselves with the West. Finland and Sweden did not have those different motives. In the beginning Finland hesitated to join because it did not want to be put in the same category as the former Warsaw Pact nations. Sweden hesitated for a different reason: the PFP smacked too much of NATO. At first Sweden wanted to make sure that Russia also joined, but in the end it joined in May 1994, on the same day as Finland and a month before Russia announced its perfunctory membership.[32]

Among the PFP members, the three Baltic states and the Eastern Europeans benefit from all five of the objectives listed above. Sweden and Finland, of course, already have democratic control of the armed forces; they are on the teaching side on that issue. But Sweden and Finland do have something to gain from the other objectives of the PFP, particularly consultation in crisis, the planning and review process, and interoperability. The provision for consultation with NATO during crises is a great innovation for the formerly neutral states, and its ramifications have not been noticed by the publics of these nations. Of course, such consultations would be automatic for both countries as members of the EU during any European crisis, but the added option of formal NATO contacts adds another dimension to the security mechanism.

The meat of the relationship, however, is the planning and review process (PARP). Through PARP, the Nordic nations go through the motions of coordinated planning and review in a manner very similar to the regular NATO planning process. Sweden, with its long tradition of planning, could adjust very easily, since the PARP will be an offspring of its regular planning process. Finland, too, has great incentives to adjust to this process.

The Individual Partnership Program (IPP) is the main vehicle of cooperation between the participating nations and NATO. Under this program, each nation agrees with NATO on a program of activities and then develops its partnership at its own pace. The partners choose from the menu set by NATO, and because each partner pays for the activities, each one can determine the pace and scope of cooperation. Because all activities are chosen from the same basic menu NATO will not be giving some nations special treatment. The PFP attempts to influence each nation equally toward a close relationship with NATO.

Finland, while not presently preparing for NATO membership, is laying the pipeline, should the Finnish leadership decide that NATO is the best option. The new F-18 Hornets that make up the Finnish Air Force provide an ideal technological champion around which much activity and training can be centered when it comes to interoperability.

Sweden is a different story. Through PARP, interoperability will gradually be reached in certain fields.[33] But because there is no perceived danger at present, the Swedes are not mentally prepared to harmonize their activities with NATO's. Unlike in Finland, the political leadership in Sweden is relaxed and lets things take their course. Given this attitude, how much Sweden will be able to accomplish under PARP is unclear. Sometimes military-political-technical developments have their own inner logic that defies political efforts to steer a situation. Essentially the public does not care and does not want to know. The activity expanded in acquiring military hardware is countered by diplomatic efforts to explain that Sweden's national security posture remains unchanged.

NATO has so far made available more than eight hundred standardization documents, which are gradually being incorporated into the military doctrines, concepts of operations, and standard operating procedures of PFP members. Over time this standardization will affect equipment requirements.

Through its exercises, which so far have been mostly rescue and peacekeeping exercises, the PFP brings the new partners together. In 1996, Sweden, Austria, and Finland together with eleven other PFP members participated in Cooperative Adventure Express '96—an exercise of the land and air forces of ten NATO members.[34] Staff officers represented the PFP nations. A major exercise in the spirit of the PFP will take place in 1997 in North Norway with participation from the Nordic nations.

CJTFs

In January 1994 NATO decided to adopt a new command and control concept: CJTFs. This model had been tested successfully during the Gulf War in 1991. CJTFs will better equip NATO military forces to handle crisis response and new peacetime operations through additional mobility and flexibility. The temporary command and control arrangements usually employed by ad hoc coalitions will be institutionalized as multinational task forces. To meet the new demands of rapid crisis response, CJTFs will be well-trained multinational forces backed by pre-established political terms of reference, standardized procedures, regular exercises, and in-place infrastructure.

The political reason behind this innovation in command and control is important. CJTFs are seen as a method by which a coalition of nations can intervene in areas of interest and yet draw upon assets belonging to NATO—i.e., assets of the United States. Although the CJTF concept seems to be tailor-made for France, France for two years essentially blocked its implementation, for reasons that involve both the issue of political control of the military forces, and turmoil and change in French politics.

Numerous internal studies have reached the conclusion that CJTFs are best achieved by augmenting three or four of NATO's major subordinate commands with extra nucleus staff that can be activated in case CJTFs are formed to go into action. The CJTFs will operate under agreed NATO standard operating procedures (SOPs) and standardization agreements (STANAGs). Non-NATO nations participating in CJTF operations will have to know these procedures in order to be efficient. Non-NATO nations contributing to a CJTF will augment the headquarters with essential liaisons and staff.

Clearly, PFP exercises and experience will be the method used to ensure that the partners learn how to fit easily into CJTFs. The capacity of any non-NATO country to operate with NATO and respond to crises in its own region will depend on the country's PFP experience and its participation in CJTFs. The most authoritative analysis of the CJTF concept to date explains this idea well:

> Because CJTFs might be employed in crises affecting PFP partners as well as NATO, the Alliance hopes that partner-states will join a "NATO-plus" CJTF operation. NATO-plus is a particularly desirable aspect of the CJTF initiative and is accorded high priority by both CJTF and PFP planners. The capability to operate together with NATO militarily is a central objective of PFP activities. As shown by the intense effort being made by partner-state forces participating in IFOR, being part of a CJTF operation is seen as a demonstration of military compatibility with NATO. Thus far 27 states have accepted the invitation to join PFP, and NATO has agreed to 16 Individual Partnership Programmes.
>
> Under PFP's Partnership Work Plans, partner militaries are exposed to NATO procedures and standards and par-

ticipate in peace-support operations, planning and exercises. In a crisis, skills honed under the PFP programme can be used in a CJTF response, effectively extending NATO's stabilising role beyond its members' territory. Even if not actually called on to deploy, the planning and capability developed under PFP and through CJTF exercises are likely to foster a greater sense of security to partner states, especially as military-to-military contacts deepen and the pool of personnel with NATO-plus CJTF experience grows.[35]

Thus an idea that was launched originally to contain France within NATO will have the effect of fostering close relations between NATO and those PFP partners that seek such relations, many of them with the purpose of ultimately joining NATO. Since Sweden and Finland have experience in international peacekeeping operations and since the soldiers are more fluent in English than those of most NATO members, their ability to utilize the new institutions is excellent.

IFOR

IFOR, led by NATO, is the best proof that events on the ground in European security have moved faster than the institutional concepts thought up by defense planners. Once the United States resolved to implement the Dayton agreement, the process of deploying IFOR was completed in two months. Sixty thousand soldiers from thirty-two nations were in place by February 1996 in one of the largest operations in Europe since WWII.[36] Through IFOR a model has been created for future operations.[37] New mechanisms for political consultations and new working relationships have been developed between NATO members and PFP partners, including as a special case Russia. There is no question that the hands-on experience of the thirty-two participating nations has proven more significant than any of the theorizing that has gone into European security institutions for the IGC opening in 1996.

For the Nordic nations, IFOR has had a profound effect. Sweden and Denmark already worked together in the NORDBAT battalions, but now for the first time a joint Nordic brigade is deployed on the European continent (Map 2.1). The battalion that Poland contributed to IFOR was at first meant to join the French division, but on Danish insistence it was included in the Nordic

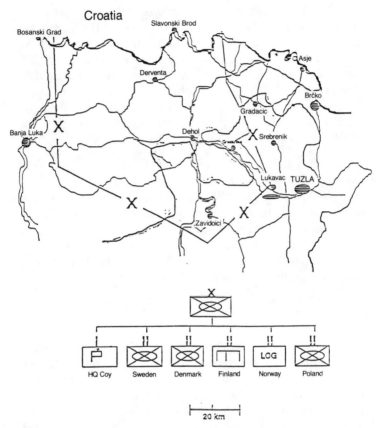

Map 2.1. Deployment of the Nordic Brigade in Bosnia

brigade instead. No doubt the newly close ties between and joint maneuvers of Denmark and Poland (and, of course, Germany) played a role in that decision.

Even more amazing from a traditional neutralist point of view is the integration of the Nordic brigade in the U.S. First Armored Division (Map 2.2). In that brigade a Swedish brigadier commands troops from both Nordic NATO members and formerly neutral Nordic states, as well as Poland, and reports to the American general who commands the First Armored Division.

The Future of the Nordic Brigade

All four Nordic nations are creating forces for international operations. Although the Norwegian and Finnish components of

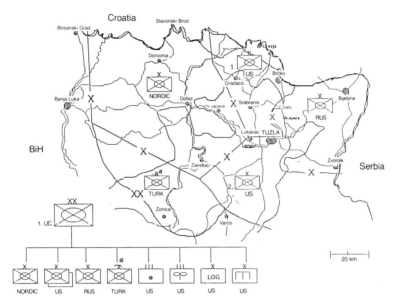

Map 2.2. Deployment of the U.S. First Armored Division in Bosnia

the Nordic Brigade in IFOR are not earmarked as international battalions, these battalions will in the future be available on a regular basis for international operations. The IFOR experience is a testing ground for Nordic military cooperation and it would be wasteful not to benefit from it.

Should the IFOR-SFOR mandate end and the troops come home there would be no need to completely dissolve the Nordic Brigade concept. Just as in the CJTF, a nucleus staff could be maintained in Denmark to coordinate and monitor future activities of the brigade. Denmark would be the natural location for such a staff, since Denmark is a member of both NATO and the EU, since NATO SOPs will be used in future operations, since the DIB will be the showcase of Nordic standing units, since Denmark is the best testing ground for training in NATO-related internationl operations, and since Denmark's special relationship with Poland and the Baltic states makes it the best base for integrating forces from these nations into the brigade.

Over time international forces in the Nordic nations could be earmarked for the brigade. All the elements that make up a potent force could easily be developed: exercises, staff work, planning, political procedures, standardization of weaponry, and airlift. A civilian staff for crisis management could be co-located with the brigade staff. If a CJTF is located at AFCENT headquarters, a liaison team from the Nordic Brigade could be attached to the CJTF staff. The brigade, with attached Baltic and Polish elements, could also participate in joint exercises with Russian forces under PFP auspices. Over time the Nordic Brigade could become an important contributor to stability in the Baltic region.

Notes

[1] Recent force structures, equipment, and plans are discussed in "Nordic Briefing," *Jane's Defence Weekly*, 24:7 (August 19, 1995), 23–35.

[2] Johan Jörgen Holst, "Norway in Search of a Nordpolitik," *Foreign Affairs* 60:1 (Fall 1981), 63–86.

[3] *Militaerbalansen 1995–96* (Oslo: Den norske Atlanterhavskomitéen, 1995), 197–200.

[4] *Forsvarskommisjonen av 1990* (Oslo: Norges offentlige utredninger, 1992), 12.

[5] Iver B Neumann and Ståle Ulriksen, "Norsk forsvars—og sikkerhetspolitikk," in Torbjörn L. Knutsen, Gunnar M. Sörby, and Sven Gherdåker, eds., *Norges utenrikspolitikk* (Bergen: Cappelan, 1995), 95.

[6] Björnar Kibsgaard, *NATOs nye kommandostruktur i nord* (Oslo: Den norske Atlanterhavskomitéen, 1993); Torkel Hovland, "NATOs nye kommandostruktur og dens betydning for Norge," *Norsk Militaert Tidskrift* 163:1 (1993), 8–15.

[7] A Norwegian lieutenant general serves as chief of staff under a British air chief marshal in AFNORTHWEST headquarters. A Norwegian major general serves as chief of staff under a British air chief marshal in AIRNORTHWEST headquarters. A Norwegian captain is represented in NAVNORTHWEST headquarters commanded by a British admiral. AFNORTH headquarters at Stavanger is commanded by a Norwegian lieutenant general with an American Air Force major general as chief of staff and a British brigadier as assistant chief of staff for joint operations.

[8] Neumann and Ulriksen, "Norsk forsvars og sikkerhets-politikk," 98.

[9] Recruitment to the batallion has been slow and was not completed until December 1996.

[10] "You cannot take it for granted that the 'project' leaders of the future in for instance Ukraine or 'project Russia' will be so familiar with poststructural 'discourse' that their haunted 'selves' will 'expose themselves' to peaceful solutions to innumerable problems with all 'the others'" (Sven H. Holtmark, "Tro ej, det mörka är betydningsfullt; just det betydningsfulla är det klara," *Internasjonal Politikk* 1 [1996], 113).

[11] See, for instance, the Navy captain Jacob Börresen, *Kystmakt: Skisse av en maritim strategi for Norge* (Oslo: Cappelan, 1993).

[12]Clive Archer, "New Threat Perceptions: Danish and Norwegian Official Views," *European Security* 3:4 (Winter 1994), 593–616.

[13]*ACCDEN news. Topic DIB. The Danish International Brigade*: Karup: Army Operational Command Denmark, July 1, 1994. The deliberations going into the decision are published in *Rapport om opstillning mv. af den internationale enhed* (Copenhagen: Ministry of Defense, July 1, 1993).

[14]*Ett modernt försvar* (Stockholm: Ministry of Defense, 1992), 10–11, 18.

[15]*Försvarsmaktstruktur 2000* (Stockholm: Defense Staff, 1988).

[16]*Programplan för det militära Försvarets utveckling 1997–2001* (Stockholm: Military Headquarters, March 4, 1996), 37.

[17]*Militaerbalansen 1995–96*, 37–8.

[18]Two hundred combat aircraft is a considerable force compared to the 300 Rafale that the French Air Force and 230 Eurofighter that the U.K. Royal Air Force are projected to have in 2015. *Defense News*, March 4–10 1996, 8.

[19]The aircraft are to be delivered by 2000 at a system cost of 14 billion FM. *Fighter Renewal Security in a Changing World* (Tikkakoski: Finnish Air Force Headquarters, October 31, 1995), 37–8. Since all manuals are in English the entire Finnish Air Force will be bilingual.

[20]*Security in a Changing World* (Helsinki: Council of State, 1995), 37–8.

[21]The cold war relationship is analyzed in Geoffrey Hill, ed., *Britain and NATO-Northern Flank* (London: Macmillan, 1988); Clive Archer, *Uncertain Trust: The British-Norwegian Defence Relationship* (Oslo: Institutt for Forsvarsstudier, 1989); and Ellmann Ellingsen, ed., *Reinforcing the Northern Flank* (Oslo: Norwegian Atlantic Committee, 1988). The Norwegian-British connection is nowhere better analyzed than in Sir James Cable, *Britain's Naval Future* (London: Macmillan, 1985), Chap. 7.

[22]Ingemar N. Dörfer, "Technology and Military Doctrine in the Future of Swedish Defense," in Ciro Elliott Zoppo, ed., *Nordic Security at the Turn of the Twenty-First Century* (New York: Greenwood, 1992). The general problem of technological dependence on larger nations is treated in "Searching for Security in a Global Economy," *Daedalus* 120:4 (Fall 1991), especially the chapter by Raymond Vernon and Ethan B. Kapstein, "National Needs, Global Resources," 1–22.

[23]Ingemar Dörfer, *System 37 Viggen. Arms Technology and the Domestication of Glory* (Oslo: Scandinavian University Press, 1973).

[24]The eleven countries were the United Kingdom, the United States, Germany, France, Norway, Denmark, Finland, Austria, Russia, Poland, and Hungary.

[25]Chap. 12, "Finland's Air Force," in Tomas Ries, *Cold Will: The Defence of Finland* (London: Brassey's, 1988).

[26]See Nikolaj Petersen, "Denmark and the New Germany, Cooperation or Adaptation"; Tomas Forsberg, "Finland und Deutschland"; and Arne Olav Brundtland, "The German Dimension in Norwegian Policy," in Burkhard Auffermann and Pekka Visuri, eds., *Nordeuropa und die deutsche Herausforderung* (Baden-Baden: Nomos Verlagsgesellschaft, 1995).

[27]In 1996 the German Navy closed down its supply depots in southern Norway.

[28]Rolf Tamnes, *The United States and the Cold War in the High North* (Oslo: Ad Notam, 1991); Mats Berdal, *The United States, Norway, and the Cold War 1954–1960* (London: Macmillan, 1997).

[29]Thirty-five percent of the Viggen and Swedish multipurpose combat aircraft (JAS) weapon systems are American. The JAS General Electric engine, like the advanced medium range air to air missiles (AMRAAM) are controlled by the U.S. Navy.

[30]When Henry Kissinger, at the height of the Vietnam War in 1972, wanted to cut off spare parts to Viggen, he was overruled by Defense Secretary Melvin Laird. See Ingemar Dörfer, *Arms Deal: The Selling of the F-16* (New York: Praeger, 1983), 183.

[31]Nick Williams, "Partnership for Peace: Permanent Fixture or Declining Asset?" *Survival* 38:1 (Spring 1996), 102.

[32]*Partnership for Peace. Presentation Document* (Stockholm: Ministry for Foreign Affairs, May 9, 1994).

[33]In the current Swedish-NATO Partnership Work Program, interoperability is sought in the following fields: fuel, flight navigation, Identification Friend Foe (IFF) liaison equipment, liaison teams, procedures, languages, terminology, position marking, map symbols, marking minefields, blood, and bunking in harbor.

[34]Cooperative Adventure Express 96 was held March 10–April 4, 1996, in Belgium and Germany. See *Atlantic News*, March 1, 1996.

[35]Charles Barry, "NATO's Combined Joint Task Forces in Theory and Practice," *Survival* 38:1 (Spring 1996), 91.

[36]The sixteen non-NATO nations contributing troops are Austria, Sweden, Finland, Hungary, the Czech Republic, Poland, Romania, Russia, Ukraine, Estonia, Latvia, Lithuania, Jordan, Egypt, Malaysia, and Morocco. (*Atlantic News*, February 20, 1996). The two largest operations in Europe were the Soviet invasion of Hungary in 1956 and the Warsaw Pact invasion of Czechoslovakia in 1968.

[37]The most comprehensive article on IFOR is "Zur neuordnung des südslawischen raumes," *Österreichische Militärische Zeitschrift* 34:2 (1996), 200–12.

Chapter 3

The Road to NATO

NATO Expansion and the North

In 1994 the Rand Corporation began a study of NATO expansion. Western governments were briefed on the study late that year and its conclusions were published in *Survival* in the spring of 1995.[1] The study concluded that there are three paths to NATO expansion: evolutionary expansion, promotion of stability, and strategic response (see Table 3.1). The first option makes the EU the driving organization; NATO membership is secondary. In the second option NATO provides the security framework necessary to anchor the new members to the West and stabilize Central Europe. The third option, strategic response, is the answer to a military threat from Russia. Table 3.2 shows the application of these three options to Northern Europe.

Promoting stability would be the best reason to admit Estonia, Latvia, and Lithuania into NATO, but that will not happen within this time span of five years. If a strategic response is called for, the Baltic states will not be admitted either because of their vulnerability in the face of a Russian threat. If evolutionary expansion works and if the Baltic states become members of the EU, they could become members of NATO in the long run.

THE BENEFITS AND COSTS OF EXPANSION

Sweden and Finland rejected the idea of NATO expansion early in 1996. Although they did not say so in public, they were op-

TABLE 3.1
ALTERNATIVE PATHS TO NATO EXPANSION

Path	Rationale	Assumptions	Timetable	Criteria	Decides	PFP
Evolutionary Expansion	Part of overall western integration	• No major security problems • ECE 'on track' • EU/NATO parallel • Avoid back-door commitments	Along with or after EU membership (ten years)	Political economic	EU and NATO ECE	Slow track
Promote Stability	Provide political/security anchor	• Security vacuum • ECE potentially unstable • NATO precedes EU	Along with or before EU membership (five years)	Political, strategic	NATO ECE	Fast track
Strategic Response	Respond to Russian threat	Expansion not needed unless Russia goes sour	Situation in Russia is catalyst	Strategic	Events in Russia	Interim step

*ECE = East-Central Europe
SOURCE: Ronald D. Asmus, Richard L. Kugler, and F. Stephen Larrabee, "NATO Expansion: The Next Step," *Survival* 37:1 (Spring 1995), 10.

TABLE 3.2
PATHS TO NATO EXPANSION IN NORTHERN EUROPE

Path	Countries	Timetable
Evolutionary expansion	Finland, Sweden	5 years
Promote stability	Poland	2 years
Strategic response	Poland, Finland, Sweden	1–2 years

posed to expansion primarily because of potential Russian reactions, and in the Swedish case also because of the possible effect on the Baltic states. Later, when the United States made clear that it was determined to go through with expansion, Prime Minister Göran Persson of Sweden changed his position, stating that he now supported NATO membership for the Baltic states. Norway also did not want NATO to expand, for fear that a wider and looser NATO would undermine the credibility of commitment and would weaken Article V for the original members. Denmark is the only Nordic nation that has supported expansion consistently, for obvious reasons. Its security situation has improved now that East Germany is in NATO and Poland is out of the Warsaw Pact. Were Poland to join NATO, the Danish situation will improve even further.

After the original discussion of expansion, NATO commissioned a study of NATO enlargement that was published in September 1995. In this entirely conventional study, the criteria for membership and the procedures for becoming a member were laid out. Given that a potential member meets the general criteria for membership, the study lists a number of elements that would ensure NATO's military credibility as it enlarges:

1. Collective Defence
   A key principle of the enlargement process is that new members will be expected not only to benefit from, but also to contribute to, the Alliance's collective defence. They should also be prepared to contribute to other Alliance missions;
2. Command Structure
   All new members should participate in an appropriate way in the command structure of the Alliance. New members joining the integrated structure will need to be integrated

into existing NATO headquarters. The Alliance will have to consider whether a limited number of new headquarters may be needed and any need for existing headquarters to cover new Areas of Responsibility. NATO operations will be controlled by existing or new NATO headquarters or, as appropriate, future CJTF headquarters;

3. Conventional Forces—Training and Exercises
New members will need to participate in NATO exercises, including those designed to ensure the common defence. Exercises should be held regularly on new members' terrritory;

4. Nuclear Forces
The supreme guarantee of the security of the Allies is provided by the strategic nuclear forces of the Alliance. New members will share the benefits and responsibilities from this in the same way as all other Allies in accordance with the Strategic Concept. New members will be expected to support the concept of deterrence and the essential role nuclear weapons play in the Alliance's strategy of war prevention as set forth in the Strategic Concept;

5. Force Structure
It is important for NATO's force structure that other Allies' forces can be deployed, when and if appropriate, on the territory of new members. The Alliance has no a priori requirement for the stationing of Alliance troops on the territory of new members. New members should participate in the Alliance's force structure. How this will be achieved may require additional considerations to include: whether new members should develop specially-trained units capable of reinforcing NATO forces and of being reinforced by NATO units; the prepositioning of materiel in critical areas; how to ensure that infrastructure is adequate to meet planned missions; and whether there is a need to increase strategic and intra-theatre mobility;

6. Intelligence
New members will have the opportunity to participate to the fullest extent possible in the NATO intelligence processes;

7. Finance
New members will be expected to contribute their share to NATO's commonly funded programmes. They should also be aware that they face substantial financial obligations when joining the Alliance;

8. Interoperability
    All new members will be expected to make every effort to
    meet NATO interoperability standards, in particular for com-
    mand, control and communication equipment. New mem-
    bers will have to incorporate NATO standard operational pro-
    cedures in selected areas, including for their national
    headquarters.[2]

A follow-on study by RAND shows that the cost of expanding
NATO to include Poland, the Czech Republic, and Hungary under ideal conditions would be low—$42 billion over a ten- to
fifteen-year period.[3] It would be immensely more costly to expand membership of the EU eastward. Poland has initiated its
own studies on this and related questions. In Sweden, on the
other hand, the defense minister in May 1995 explicitly forbade
the parliamentary committee exploring the next five-year defense
plan to study the problem.[4] As a consequence, the liberal and
conservative members left the committee, to return only in January 1996. In Finland an internal study in the fall of 1995 reached
the conclusion that Finland should not attempt to join NATO for
the time being, for reasons including the effects on Northern
European stability, uncertainty regarding NATO's future, the
geopolitical situation of Finland, the desire not to provoke Russia,
and the costs.[5]

Of all the formerly neutral European states Switzerland has
published the most extensive study of the consequences of NATO
membership.[6] This study concludes that Switzerland would be
welcome in NATO, since it would make a considerable contribution. Its contribution to collective defense and crisis management
could include the assignment of squadrons of F/A-18 fighters or
of mechanized brigades equipped with upgraded Leopard 2
tanks and adapted to the C^3I standards of NATO.[7] Only if Switzerland were to participate in a multinational corps would its
military have to be integrated into the military structure of
NATO. Another welcome Swiss contribution to NATO could be
large transport aircraft, namely the C-17, which is in high demand in Europe. As a consequence of NATO membership the
Army units committed to NATO would have a higher share of
professional soldiers and the Army as a whole would be down-
sized because of increased costs. The Swiss contribution to NA-
TO's infrastructure would be marginal, around $100 million per
year. A final benefit of NATO membership would be integration

into NATO's early warning and control system and the improved national air defense system that would result. Were it not for the resistance of the public, concludes the study, Swiss membership in NATO could be achieved rapidly, smoothly, and inexpensively.

An Austrian study is much more concentrated on the diplomatic aspects of NATO expansion and its consequences for Austria. It reaches the conclusion that Austria should join NATO to stabilize the European security situation.[8]

The official study on NATO enlargement shows that Sweden and Finland are eminently qualified for membership; the Swiss study shows that the transition into the alliance would be smooth. In 1997 the negotiations will start with the first candidates—most likely Poland, the Czech Republic, and Hungary. Before the turn of the century NATO will have new members in Central Europe.

IMPLICATIONS OF POLISH MEMBERSHIP IN NATO

Of the Nordic nations only Denmark would welcome Poland into NATO; Denmark would like to see another member of the alliance placed between itself and Russia, with the accompanying benefits in conventional defense, air defense, and naval superiority in the Baltic Sea. Danish cooperation with Poland, already begun in the early 1990s, could take place within the framework of a tested alliance. Polish democracy and civic institutions would be strengthened through NATO membership.

Should Poland join, the three Baltic states will at first feel singled out as having been left on the wrong side of the division of Europe. Depending on NATO's posture in Poland, Russia may feel provoked and could take counteractions in the Baltic. Most likely, a low foreign-troop presence with emphasis on reinforcement and infrastructure in Poland will be militarily beneficial to the Baltic states. In a real crisis, Western support of the Baltic states will be easier to implement if Poland is in NATO.

Finland currently sees no advantage in Polish membership since it could provoke Russia to take a harder stance in the Baltic region. If Russia absorbs the thought of Polish (and Czech, and Hungarian) membership over the next few years, Finland could benefit from having a more "Western" Poland nearby. Since Finland is much more qualified to join NATO than is Poland, the idea of Finnish membership, dormant within the Finnish elite, could surface. In seven years' time it would be in harmony with the argument of evolutionary expansion.

A recent poll examined how citizens of the three Western European powers view NATO expansion (see Table 3.3).

Sweden has only recently given thought to the implications of expanded NATO membership in Europe. Should Poland join there is a fait accompli and the Swedish argument concerning the situation of the Baltic states is overtaken by events. Polish membership in itself would not affect the arguments of the Swedish elite, but if Polish membership led to Finnish membership the situation would be radically different. Sweden's position as a nonaligned island in the middle of the EU and between Finland, Norway, and Denmark will look increasingly precarious, especially since Sweden's absence from NATO would complicate the defense situation for Finland and Norway. Briefly put, should Finland decide to join NATO it will be extraordinarily difficult for Sweden not to follow.

Codeword NATO

Western Integration by Default?

Since 1994, Finland and Sweden have participated in a myriad of national security meetings, actions, and consultations with the Western nations in the UN, the OSCE, and the WEU, and,

TABLE 3.3
PUBLIC RESPONSES IN BRITAIN, FRANCE, AND GERMANY TO
POSSIBLE NATO EXPANSION

		Britain	France	Germany
Poland	favor	79%	68%	61%
	oppose	16	24	36
Hungary	favor	70	63	79
	oppose	21	26	25
Czech Republic	favor	64	58	60
	oppose	28	30	36
Baltics	favor	56	57	52
	oppose	32	29	40

SOURCE: United States Information Agency, *The New European Security Architecture* (Washington DC: USIA Office of Research and Media Reaction, September 1995), 15.

through the PFP, also in NATO. In IFOR a Nordic brigade under Swedish command is integrated into the U.S. First Armored Division. Will Finland and Sweden thus be able to slip into NATO unobtrusively, without anyone noticing? The answer has to be no.

The four functions of NATO were defined at the Rome summit in 1991:

- to act as one foundation of stability in Europe;
- to be the forum for political transatlantic consultation;
- to constitute the primary mechanism to deter and defend against attacks on its members; and
- to preserve the strategic balance in Europe.[9]

NATO provides public goods in the security field for Finland and Sweden. It provides stability and preserves the strategic balance for both nations. It probably deters attack on these two nations now as it has in the past. But Finland and Sweden do not participate in the political transatlantic consultations. They do participate in the consultations of the UN, the OSCE, and the EU, but the first two of these institutions are increasingly losing their clout in European security, and the common defense and security policy of the EU has so far dealt only with peripheral issues.

In European security the United States and the three European powers make the decisions, but NATO will at least let the smaller nations in on the decision-making process. France, which used to have an interest in keeping some Europeans out of NATO in order to have alternative forums for its diplomacy, has now changed its mind. The high cost of defense, the perceived mediocre quality of its weaponry compared to that of the United States, and its marginalization in vital European security matters have persuaded France to abandon the WEU and Eurocorps as major projects and instead attempt to take the lead in NATO Europe. This attitude is welcomed by Washington in light of the decline of the United Kingdom and the self-imposed limits of German military power in Europe. Thus, given that NATO is the only viable security institution in Europe, if Finland and Sweden are to have an influence consummate to their considerable achievements, they must join NATO.

In Finland such a decision would be taken by the security elite as a result of a changed Russian threat perception. Through the PFP all the preparations for membership will have been made, and the public will be presented with a fait accompli. The president and the entire government will claim the privilege of serving the national interest best by joining the West. In this situation the nation will stand almost totally united.

In Sweden, however, joining NATO is a major decision that may well have to be based on a referendum. Current opinion polls indicate a significant shift in favor of NATO. In 1996, 55 percent of the population wanted intensified cooperation with NATO, 13 percent immediately and 42 percent later.[10] Despite occasional arguments in leading liberal newspapers there has been no formal debate in Sweden on NATO membership. This study is not about debates or domestic politics in the Nordic nations. It is about the correlation of forces, the impact of institutions and the logic of events in European security policy.

To understand the Swedish mindset, one has to realize where the Swedes are coming from. In 1994, a commission appointed by the Bildt government reported on Swedish clandestine relations with the West during the cold war. An officious booklet published by the Ministry of Defense summarized the findings:

> There was in the 1950s a common Swedish understanding that Sweden, if attacked by the Soviet Union as a part of a major war, could be capable of effective resistance for a short period only, say a couple of months. At the same time such a major war was by no means seen as an unlikely scenario. The political leadership, i.e., the government with the full understanding of the leaders of the non-socialist opposition parties, therefore took certain unilateral measures in order to facilitate prompt military assistance from the US or the UK, should the need arise in the context of a European war. The existence of such preparations has recently been revealed in the report of the Neutrality Policy Commission, which presented its findings to the Prime Minister in February 1994.
>
> Such measures were of a delicate nature in the perspective of the limited scope for manoeuvre in Swedish security policy, as stated publicly by the Government during the 1950s. The Government had then ruled out military staff deliberations or common defence plans with other nations. Some military "technical" measures in a more narrow sense were, however, implicitly accepted. The strategy and the overall perspective of the physical measures were kept strictly secret and were known only to a very small circle of people at the highest level.

Provided Sweden continued to care about its defence, the Swedish authorities were fairly confident that the national military forces would be at least temporarily sufficient for that part of a defence campaign which would take place on Swedish territory. Besides, our capability to strike from the air against a sea-borne invasion fleet was being substantially strengthened. What was still lacking was the capacity to strike against Soviet base areas on the other side of the Baltic, used for an attack on Sweden. The priority targets in this context would be air bases, naval base areas, and harbours, i.e., "strategic" targets. The primary potential supplier of such missions would no doubt have been the US Strategic Air Command—"with or without nuclear weapons"—or possibly the Royal Air Force Bomber Command.

Sweden therefore took a number of limited steps in order to improve the possibilities for efficient and early "strategic" assistance from the West, should that be needed in a war situation. High level military missions were prepared to be sent to some capitals in a crisis situation. A small number of reliable communication links were established, creating a potential for a limited exchange of staff information or air control data. Some Swedish airfields were adapted for heavy bomber landings, primarily for aircraft in distress. The Air Force also prepared for the installation of a US/UK Identification-Friend-or-Foe (IFF) system.

On the whole, the Swedish measures were taken on a unilateral national basis, and there is nothing to indicate the existence of any kind of general agreement with the United States in military assistance in war. But US documents now available, in particular the National Security Council policy decisions of the period, show that the United States intended coming to Sweden's assistance in the event of war, in order to forestall a Soviet control of Swedish territory.[11]

Despite its sensational findings this report evoked only slight interest. Some maintained, against their better judgment, that they had known all along. Some expressed outrage because they had not been told the truth. But most did not react at all and continued to think that Sweden throughout the cold war had been a beacon of solid neutrality between East and West. The conclusions of the commission report simply did not sink in. Thus the true history of Swedish security policy during the cold war is not yet understood by the Swedes themselves, and anyone arguing that the step from informal to formal NATO membership is a small one will have a hard time convincing them.

The debate if it comes will more likely focus on the functions of the new NATO. All international military operations after the cold war in Europe have been Petersberg operations—peacekeeping, search and rescue missions, and humanitarian aid. Sweden and Finland have participated in such missions, most recently under NATO command in IFOR. Meanwhile, Article V has become a red banner because very few have bothered to study it. It states, "The Parties agree that an armed attack against one or more of them in Europe or North America shall be considered an attack against them all; and consequently they agree that, if such an armed attack occurs, each of them, in exercise of the right of individual or collective self defence recognised by Article 51 of the Charter of the United Nations, will assist the Party or Parties so attacked by taking forthwith, individually and in concert with the other Parties, such action as it deems necessary, including the use of armed force, to restore and maintain the security of the North Atlantic area."[12] During the cold war, when a clear and present danger existed, the response was obvious and immediate. The NATO command structure and the layer-cake defense of the central front in Germany gave any response an automatic momentum that no one could escape. One for all and all for one was the solution. The American nuclear umbrella, encompassing all its European allies, was the strategic glue that kept the military alliance together. The political glue had been set at the signing of the North Atlantic Treaty in April 1949: the shared experience, aspirations, and expectations of the Western democracies.

But after the cold war Article V lends itself to a looser interpretation: "Each [party] . . . will assist the Party . . . attacked by taking forthwith . . . such action as it deems necessary." Greece rushing to the defense of Norway? Turkey supporting Denmark in a meaningful manner? What really counts is the American, and increasingly the German, commitment. The risk of watering down Article V and thereby loosening the American commitment is why NATO expansion is resisted by some nations. Yet as Philip Zelikow put it, "The United States has never gone to war because of a preexisting treaty of alliance. Such a treaty would only serve to codify and announce a readiness to shed blood that had already been manifested unmistakenly by other deeds."[13]

If a debate occurs the Swedish government will portray NATO activities as Petersberg activities. A looser interpretation of Article V will be given to the public, emphasizing the ceremonies that go with the reporting to the Security Council and the response of the UN. Of course if the European security situation is grave, the major Western powers will see through such verbiage and might veto an eventual Swedish application to join NATO. But no matter what language is used in the internal Swedish debate, no matter what hidden motives lurk behind a decision to join, the West will calculate its own interests. If Sweden offers a substantial net contribution to Western security, as it presently does, it will be admitted.

NORDIC COOPERATION

The negotiations on a Scandinavian Defense Union between Sweden, Norway, and Denmark in 1948–49 failed because Sweden and Norway had different conceptions of that union.[14] Sweden saw it as a genuine independent bloc outside the cold war, boosted by modern defense equipment from the Western powers. Norway, on the other hand, saw it as a subregional part of the Western alliance—the three Scandinavian nations working together under the overall leadership of Washington and London. As a result the negotiations failed and Norway and Denmark, together with Iceland, were among the founding members of NATO.

As recent investigations have shown, Sweden continued to maintain intimate and clandestine contacts with Oslo and Copenhagen through personal contacts among leading officers and special lines of communications with U.S. Air Force headquarters at Wiesbaden.[15] It is still unclear how long these contacts persisted, or if they ever stopped. Had there been a war these preparations would have been woefully inadequate for efficient coordination of the war effort, but the preparations left no doubt in the West (and the East) on whose side Sweden wanted to be. Throughout this period Finland was chained by its special treaty with the Soviet Union.[16]

After the cold war the Nordic alternative has again been presented. The most prominent supporter is former Swedish commander in chief Bengt Gustafsson, who beginning in the summer of 1992 (while he still was in office) began to plead for more Nordic cooperation. The European security system based on the EU would be fragile and lack credibility when it came to the Nordic nations, he claimed.[17] He met little support in the governments of the four Nordic countries, including his own. But in the spring of 1996 three veteran Finnish diplomats published a study wherein they pleaded for Finnish-Swedish coordination in defense policy. Aware of the failure to do so in the 1930s, they claimed that the time was now ripe for another try.[18]

In fact Nordic cooperation in the defense field has increased since 1989. The regular meetings of defense ministers that earlier had only UN peacekeeping operations on the agenda now touch upon every aspect of security. Cooperation in the creation of the Baltic Peacekeeping Battalion (BALTBAT) is one example. The development of the Nordic battalions in the former Yugoslavia into the Nordic Brigade in IFOR is the most spectacular example, and it may become a permanent institution in Nordic security. A treaty on cooperation in procurement was signed in December 1994, and the staffs and armament directors are defining future joint projects. Independent of such cooperation the Nordic nations have bought weapons from each other, mostly from Sweden. Given the cost of weapons systems such as the JAS Sweden will have to cooperate to a much higher degree in the future. The potential partners in cooperations in armaments are all European and American. As an outsider to the WEU Sweden can become a member of the Western European Armaments Group (WEAG) only through special arrangements. As an outsider to NATO, Sweden, which has the fifth largest defense industry in Western Europe, will be at a considerable disadvantage in the future.

The Norwegian political scientist Iver Neumann has seen where Nordic cooperation can lead:

> [The] Partnership for Peace is about adjustment to the joint Commands that already exist within NATO. If you assume that this work has the purpose to create a geographically extended command structure under one or several hats, the route of incremental steps will maybe lead to a situation where Norway, Sweden and Finland have the opportunity to create a joint command within this structure. The work to give some substance to the Combined Joint Task Forces points in this direction even if other tendencies also appear. . . . Such a situation would also lead to Danish inter-

est to participate. The dimensions of security cooperation in the North thus created would be of a larger . . . magnitude altogether than those currently discussed in the public debate. This is one of several possibilities. If you look for a grand strategy for security policy cooperation between Norway, Sweden, Finland and also Denmark this is the only possibility. For this strategy as for the general question of a place in the new European order it is however the political will to take the incremental steps that counts—that secures the central position in Europe that many but not all see as the very point of security policy.[19]

Neumann has seen the implications, but his road of incremental steps is smoother than in real life. Nordic cooperation has in the postwar world been a code word for two interest groups in the nations of the North—the neutralists who do not like NATO, and the Westerners, particularly in Sweden, who want more cooperation with the NATO nations Norway and Denmark. Just as in 1948–49, Nordic cooperation in the security field implies a NATO, in particular an Anglo-Saxon, connection via Norway. As little as in the 1940s the Nordic nations can by themselves form a viable security bloc. The incremental steps will go a long way, but not all the way. Neither the publics of the Nordic nations nor the major Western powers will be satisfied with a halfway house of Nordic security. When the moment of truth arrives Finland and Sweden will have to make a clear decision to join NATO or not, just as they decided to join the EU.

The Decline and Fall of the WEU

In the North the WEU has been a false start all along. Denmark, a founding member of NATO and an old member of the EU, has refused to join the WEU and is only an observer.[20] Norway, having rejected EU membership, is an associate. Sweden and Finland, together with Austria, knew that they should not apply for WEU membership when they joined the EU.[21] Since the WEU defense guarantees are stronger than NATO's and since the United States through NATO has guaranteed to defend those WEU members that are members of NATO, it is not possible to achieve U.S. guarantees via the back door, i.e., by joining the WEU without joining NATO.

In the aftermath of German unification, German Chancellor Helmut Kohl and French President François Mitterrand in October 1991 launched a much more ambitious goal for the WEU. They proposed increased cooperation on arms with a view to establishing a European Arms Agency, forming military units under the authority of the WEU, creating the French-German army unit, Eurocorps, and establishing the WEU as a component of the EU's common foreign and security policy. Over the next few years the achievements of the WEU were small, however. It helped enforce the economic embargo against Serbia, it quarantined Serbia in the Adriatic, and it policed Mostar. At a meeting at Petersberg (outside Bonn) in June 1992, it was decided that the WEU should engage in peacekeeping, search and rescue missions, and humanitarian aid. Military combat was mentioned as an afterthought, but because the other missions were highlighted they became known as Petersberg missions and were set in contrast to Article V missions of NATO—i.e., military combat in support of an ally.

Had the WEU been limited to Petersberg missions as Britain wished, the new members of the EU would not have had difficulties in joining. But since France and Germany wanted to use the WEU to create a European capability to act in situations when the United States was unwilling or unable to act, this option was never a real one. The unraveling of the WEU in fact if not in theory came about as a consequence of the French change of mind.[22] In January 1993 it was established that the French forces in Eurocorps were also to come under NATO command should that be necessary. In IFOR a French division is under NATO command for the first time since 1966, when Charles de Gaulle asked NATO to leave Paris for Brussels. France, beginning with Prime Minister Edouard Balladur and continuing with President Jacques Chirac, has realized that the WEU cannot achieve what an organization that defends Europe must do:

- protection of the home land,
- the organization of adequate forces,
- joint production and procurement of defense equipment, and
- coordination of defense and security policies with foreign policy.[23]

In addition such an organization must have sea- and airlift, and C^3I, including satellites, all of which is now provided by the United States at a cost of tens of billions of dollars annually. According to the Royal United Services Institute of London it would cost the Europeans $108 billion a year to replace the American assets devoted to NATO.[24]

Since France realized that the other WEU nations were unwilling to fund French defense expenditures through the WEU, since France had to cut its own defense budget, since the Gulf War had shown that French military equipment was not up to the standard of the American military, and since France, like Britain and Germany, lacked the infrastructure and means for good strategic mobility and C^3I, France decided that the best way to play a role again was in NATO.[25] In December 1995 Foreign Minister Hervé de la Charette rejoined the alliance's Military Committee. The WEU had thus achieved its most important transitional function.

Almost totally independent of these developments, the European nations preparing for the IGC beginning in March 1996 established their positions for that conference.[26] Here the position of Britain differs from that of France and Germany. But the debate will not be resolved; no matter how intricate a solution is devised, the WEU will again be relegated to the sidelines and NATO will remain the only important defense (as opposed to security) organization. Because the European powers cannot get their act together Sweden and Finland may again escape their moment of truth. They can find solace in the nuances of IGC lingo simply because there is no sense of urgency in European security policy.

THE WEU-EU RELATIONSHIP

One of the main security issues on the IGC agenda is the relationship between the EU and the WEU. Article J-4 of the Maastricht Treaty outlines this relationship: "1. The common foreign and security policy shall include all questions related to the security of the European Union, including the eventual framing of a common defense policy, which might in time lead to a common defense. 2. The Union requests the WEU which is an integral part of the European Union, to elaborate and implement decisions and actions of the Union which have defense implications." This loosely worded treaty will have to be put into action during and after the 1996 conference. Orthodox NATO nations such as the United Kingdom will not allow the WEU to be integrated fully into the EU. Rather, London will suggest that WEU and EU meetings be held back-to-back in the future, maintaining the distinction between the two institutions.[27]

Finland and Sweden, who originally backed the British position, have tabled a proposal designed to enhance the competence of the EU in conflict management by including humanitarian and rescue operations, peacekeeping, and crisis management—i.e., Petersberg tasks—in the EU's mandate. They want to revise Article J-4.2 to reinforce the link between the EU and the WEU regarding the implementation of military crisis management decisions adopted by the EU within the scope of the common foreign and security policy (CFSF). According to the proposed revisions all the contributing EU member states will participate on an equal footing in planning and decision-making related to operations enacted by the EU. The WEU is expected to adopt a declaration to this end. The EU member states are encouraged to provide information about the forces they have available for such EU-enacted and WEU-conducted operations. No capability will be created within the EU for planning, organizing, or using military resources: "In joint military crisis management, the member states of the [European] Union will engage resources which are under national and/or common (alliance) authority and jurisdiction for operations decided upon by the [EU] and implemented by the WEU. When taking such decisions, appropriate consultation will be needed with other international institutions (NATO). Voluntary decisions on committing and contributing forces will take place in accordance with the respective constitutional [e.g., parliamentary approval] and institutional rules [including CJTF]."[28] Thus, Finland and Sweden are prepared to go a long way to perform Petersberg tasks, and for this purpose they are willing to create a stronger link between the EU and the WEU than the United Kingdom would prefer.

This view clashes with that of France and Germany, who want the EU and the WEU to include all tasks—i.e., also collective defense.[29] Their penchant for order makes them believe that no loose ends should remain in West European security. Thus full members of the EU—i.e., Sweden, Finland, and Austria—should also belong to the WEU security area. As Karl Kaiser puts it,

> In considering potential contingencies relevant to the self-defence of the EU, *the zone to be covered by its policy of self-defence* must first be defined. It is important that such a

definition should include not only those countries with full membership of WEU (covered by the security guarantee of Article V of the modified Brussels Treaty). It must also include other EU members, as well as all those European democracies that are associated with the EU through the kind of agreements that are eventually to lead to their full membership, and non-EU European members of NATO. As these countries, especially those in Eastern Central Europe, re-enter the community of democracies and free-market economies which are linked by common values and a common culture, their security will become a vital interest of the EU. It is an illusion to believe that the security of the EU itself would not be profoundly affected if the security of these countries were put at risk.

There is of course a difference, depending on whether a country is covered by a formal alliance guarantee, or whether it merely forms *de facto* a part of the security zone with which the EU is connected through links of solidarity, interests, common values, and a multitude of political and economic factors. On the one hand, the EU must retain its ability to act pragmatically rather than automatically as long as these countries are not parties to formal alliance treaties. But on the other hand, it is clearly in the EU's interest not to allow the impression of a second-rate security area to be formed in future member countries. The EU/WEU must avoid this by underpinning its *implicit commitment to the security and defence of the EU security zone as a whole* by increasingly deepening economic, political, societal and military links.[30]

Since the United Kingdom and the United States will not permit WEU membership without NATO membership, logic spells NATO membership for the three formerly neutral European states. Yet the debate over NATO expansion centers completely on Central and Eastern Europe. It seems that the major European powers have not bothered to think things through. The WEU issue is discussed in one forum and the question of NATO expansion in a totally different forum. Yet the two are intimately connected.[31] The Berlin summit of June 1996 strengthened both the European defense indentity within NATO and the concept of CJTFs. Both decisions suit Sweden and Finland just fine; they underline the fact that NATO remains the sole serious security organization in Europe.

If the confusion persists, and if Finland and Sweden insist on muddling through, they stand to lose diplomatic good will. If they constantly squabble about the theology of non-alignment, they may end up marginalized. Their saving grace is the professionalism of their representatives, which gives them a reputation as serious people. If, on the other hand, the WEU is going nowhere and NATO continues to be the only meaningful security organization in Europe, Finland, and Sweden will fare better. The Nordic Brigade in Bosnia under American command is the supreme test case. Neither the UN, the OSCE, nor the WEU is running this operation—NATO is. In fact, as long as Norway stays outside the EU, a WEU-run Nordic brigade with Norwegian participation will be complicated to field. Since there is no need for a CJTF, NATO will likely command such operations, as long as the Swedes and the Finns go along. The Nordic Brigade in Bosnia, under a U.S. division commander with a Danish brigade commander and a Swedish chief of staff, is the ideal tool to develop integration in the field. Since the WEU has not yet established structures, since not even Denmark is a full member of the WEU, and since the military-political instincts of the Northern nations are Anglo-Saxon rather than continental, the WEU/EU question can be resolved as long as the major European powers do not insist on EU purity. If they do so insist, NATO membership is the simplest solution, since it will lead to full membership in the WEU and thereby full participation in all the EU's decision-making processes.

The Baltic Dimension

"Whereas the East European satellites possessed at least the formal attributes of independent statehood, however theoretical they may have been, the Baltic states lacked their own currencies, armed forces, border guards, diplomatic services, central or even local banks, railways, airlines, and even tourist offices." [32]

In August 1991 the three Baltic republics—Estonia, Latvia, and Lithuania—restored their independence. Since 1940 they had been occupied, first by Nazi Germany and then by the Soviet Union; millions had been deported or killed; and millions of Russians had settled in the three states, which altogether count eight million inhabitants. Leading Western powers such as the United States and the United Kingdom had never recognized the Soviet incorporation of the Baltic states, but others, including their Nordic neighbors, had done exactly that. Thus a sense of guilt has permeated the actions of the Nordic nations, especially Sweden, since the end of the cold war.

Denmark took the initial lead in supporting the Baltic quest for independence in 1990. As Danish defense minister Hans Haekkerup put it years later,[35] "Denmark regards the UN, NATO and OSCE as the cornerstones of our security policy. . . . In addition to these multinational commitments, however, we have found that the area where Denmark as an individual nation can make a difference is in our own neighborhood, the Baltic region."[33] Danish support has been particularly strong when it comes to military assistance, both with BALTBAT and bilateral assistance.

But it was the Bildt government of Sweden that from October 1991 made its special task the improvement of the security situation of the Baltic and thereby of Sweden, as well. Sweden offered its services in the intricate negotiations for Russian troop withdrawal from the Baltics, a feat that was accomplished by August 1993 in Lithuania and by August 1994 in Estonia and Latvia. During a period of two and a half years (February 1992–August 1994), Swedish diplomats acted as intermediaries and expediters in the withdrawal process. Although the Bush administration at first had its attention focused elsewhere—namely, on the protection of Mikhail Gorbachev's position—the unification of Germany and the Gulf War. The Clinton administration coming into power in January 1993 encouraged the Swedish quiet diplomacy and laid the groundwork with Moscow while the three Baltic states themselves worked out the details. Because of its special ties with Estonia, Finland was also involved, as was the strongly supportive Denmark.

Once the Russian troops had left their shores in August 1994 the Baltic states were able to act as normal European nations. Like the other nations of East-Central Europe, their desire is to forge strong ties to the West in defense and diplomacy. But their history and geographical location make the Baltic states different from the other post-communist states of Europe.

DEFENSE

Conventional wisdom has it that the Baltic states are indefensible, given their proximity to Russian military power and their small size. Unlike Finland they did not resist Soviet and German military attacks in 1940–41; to do so would have been futile. Thus at best a trip-wire defense is achievable for the Baltics, a force that will prevent Russia from again taking over the nations quietly without causing an international crisis.

Carl Bildt has aptly cast the Baltic states as a litmus test for Russian behavior in European security.[34] Thus new armed forces have been established and trained in Estonia with the particular support of Finland and in Latvia and Lithuania with the additional support of Sweden and Denmark. BALTBAT has been conceived and supported by several European nations, including Britain, Germany, France, the Netherlands, and the Nordic nations. The United States, too, participates in the work on BALTBAT, which is coordinated from Denmark. While the creation of BALTBAT will allow troops from the three Baltic nations to participate alongside the NATO members in future peacekeeping missions (they all contribute to IFOR, for instance), the real purpose is to create in each state a national trip-wire force with knowledge of NATO and its procedures.

Although the Nordic nations until recently have refused to sell arms to the Baltic nations, they have contributed radar equipment, coast guard vessels, and other components of infrastructure.

DIPLOMACY

Since the defense dimension of Baltic security can yield only limited results, the diplomatic dimension is the more important. At the Copenhagen meeting of the EU in June 1993 it was established that all European democracies are welcome into the EU if they meet the other criteria for membership. Since 1995, the three Baltic states have enjoyed special Europe agreements with the EU, and Sweden and Finland have championed their cause for early membership in the IGC. As Bildt put it in January 1995, "Both the former and the present Swedish government have declared that we regard the eastern enlargement of the EU as a crucially important issue and that the Baltic countries must be given the possibility of membership on the same terms and at the same time as the Central European states. To secure that this will indeed happen is one of the most important—and most demanding—tasks for Sweden foreign policy over the next few years." [35]

Others are not so optimistic. The RAND study on NATO expansion, for instance, singles out Estonia as a serious EU candidate member together with the Central Europeans.[36] Latvia and Lithuania are not yet ready for EU membership, according to the RAND analysis. The IGC may decide otherwise, but even under the best of circumstances the most suitable EU candidate—the Czech Republic—will not be a member before 2000.[37] The Baltic states are further down the list and it is unlikely that their precarious security situation will allow them to jump the queue.

To join the European family of good democracies the Russian minority problem in Estonia and Latvia must be controlled. In Estonia and Latvia, Russians form a large part of the population (see Table 3.4). Harsh citizenship laws have not alleviated the situation, even if emissaries from the OSCE have set the record straight. The uneasy coexistence between natives and Russians is one factor that might endanger the stability of these new nations in the future. The unresolved border dispute between Estonia and Russia is another irritating element.

Soft security—migration, crime, pollution, and unsafe nuclear reactors—is the imminent problems for the Baltic states in the shadow of postcommunist Russia. But like the other former communist states of Central and Eastern Europe they have chosen to join the PFP and they all want to join NATO. Lithuania applied for membership in January 1994 when the PFP was launched, and the others have followed suit. The reaction of the main NATO powers to the possibility of expansion has been cautious. The consensus among them is that the Baltic states cannot be defended conventionally and that a nuclear guarantee extended to

TABLE 3.4
NATIONALITIES OF RESIDENTS OF THE BALTIC STATES, 1989

	Total population	Native	Russian	Polish	Other
Estonia	1,566,000	62	30	—	8
Latvia	2,667,000	52	34	—	14
Lithuania	3,675,000	80	9	7	4

SOURCE: Kristian Gerner and Stefan Hedlund, *The Baltic States and the End of the Soviet Empire* (London: Routledge, 1993), 74.

them would lack credibility in Moscow and thereby be self-defeating. Thus early or even medium-term NATO membership is simply not in the cards.

Although Finland and Denmark have not commented on the issue of Baltic membership, the Swedish response has been confused. One standard line has been that NATO should not expand at all since this would create new divisions in Europe and leave the Baltic states out in the cold. The reactions of Poland, the Czech Republic, and Hungary to this free advice by a formerly neutral state is easy to predict. Over time, however, the Swedish government has come to give verbal support to Baltic membership in NATO. Bolder still was the recommendation of Carl Bildt, in 1995, who maintained that the Baltic states should be made NATO members, just as they wished.[38] Since Bildt does not yet advocate NATO membership for his own country, the recommendation may seen gratuitous, but as *realpolitik* it does make sense. Obviously the security situation of Sweden—and Finland—would improve if the Baltic states not only were free of Russian troops but belonged to NATO as well.

Although the three Baltic nations will not be able to join NATO in this century, they may well join the EU and thereby drastically improve their security situation, just as Finland did in 1995. They would improve their situation further if they could learn how to cooperate on defense, security, and diplomatic issues. At present they seldom do.[39]

The Nordic Role

After the cold war a major Swedish security interest was to consolidate the security of the newly liberated Baltic states. In an effort to earn its keep in Washington and win the respect of Brussels while it negotiated its entry into the EU, the Bildt government decided to franchise Baltic security for the West.[40] Although remarkably successful in practice, some of the theory and rhetoric connected with the Swedish effort has led to misunderstandings, and if pursued further, the effort could backfire. Least troublesome are American scholars, who in well-meaning treatises urge Sweden to take the lead in the historic task of securing the Baltic.[41] Far more troublesome is the German point of view, repeated during 1995 by Defense Minister Volker Rühe, that the Nordic nations take responsibility for security demands of the Baltic states.[43] These German pronouncements can be attributed to inadequate attention paid to Northern Europe, false logic, and to some extent wrong signals from Sweden, which for a period claimed that it would not stand idly by if any of the Baltic states were subject to agression.

In the spring of 1996 two more instances of Western misapprehension surfaced. In his Alastair Buchan Memorial Lecture at the International Institute for Strategic Studies in London, Douglas Hurd stated, "Because NATO existed Finland, and to an even greater extent, Sweden, have been able to live free and independent during the years of the Cold War. It should not be impossible to construct some form of Baltic security system to which these two countries and the three Baltic states would belong. They would have direct collective dealings with both NATO and Russia." [43] This idea was developed further in an article published by some of the authors behind the original RAND study on NATO expansion. [44] This new article proposed a strategy based on five pillars: (1) strengthening Baltic reform; (2) nordic-Baltic cooperation; (3) EU enlargement; (4) keeping the door open for NATO membership; and (5) dealing with Moscow. This is an excellent strategy in most of its components. But when it comes to the Finnish and Swedish contributions the authors misjudge the position of these nations in the European security concert:

> Many commentators in these countries suggest that they are already providing significant amounts of assistance and can hardly be expected to do more. But the Baltic issue is arguably the key national security issue facing these countries in the years ahead. Preserving that gain in security and strategic depth must logically be the top national security priority for these countries, and resource decisions should be restructured accordingly. Against this background, it should be possible for them to find additional resources, especially if they concentrate and coordinate their efforts. [45]

Contrary to that statement, the integration of Sweden and Finland into Western structures is the top national security interest of these nations. The Baltic states are important but not vital interests for Sweden and Finland. The stubborn resistance of Sweden and Finland to NATO membership has been taken at face value by the West, which has drawn the logical conclusion and suggested other arrangements. Finland, nowadays does not at all want to be considered a bridge between East and West.

Unlike Sweden, Finland participates in the process of consultations between NATO and prospective new members, although Finnish membership is not on the horizon. The reorganization of the U.S. State Department, in which the five Nordic nations and the three Baltic nations are now grouped together in one bureau has also encouraged the thought of a neutral Baltic-Nordic group.

In 1919–21 Finland carried out a policy of *Randstaatspolitik*, negotiating a mutual defense agreement with Poland, Estonia, and Latvia. The agreement however, was, not ratified by the Finnish parliament and the foreign minister was forced to resign over it. After seventy years of Soviet domination Finland is finally in the clear as a respected and valuable member of the EU, a crucial stepping stone to the West. Would Finland be willing to join an international security club, headed by Sweden, whose other members are a militarily weak Denmark and the three Baltic states, which by their very location could invite trouble? No matter how much verbal patronage such a club were given by Washington and Bonn, Finland certainly is not willing to face Moscow alongside only the Nordic and Baltic states, when it has just secured the ability to face Moscow with the support of the entire EU. Nordic support of the Baltic states will be far-reaching in fair weather. It will stop the moment anything vaguely resembling Article V conditions appears on the scene.

For obvious reasons neither the United States, Germany, nor Britain, not to mention France, has paid much attention to security in the Baltic area since the end of the cold war. The suggestions of Volker Rühe in 1995 and Douglas Hurd in 1996 that Finland, Sweden, and the three Baltic nations should form a Baltic security system shows the cavalier fashion in which the topic is dismissed. Neither the Nordic nations nor the Baltic states are interested in a regionalization of Baltic security. The idea of franchising security for the West was conceived by Sweden in the early 1990s. But franchising, then as now, assumes that there is a main contractor.

In August 1996 Sweden confirmed in Washington that it would take the lead on soft security issues in the Baltic region. According to this school of thought Sweden and Finland will remain outside NATO as long as Russian-Baltic relations develop normally. This is a revival of the Nordic balance idea from the cold war. But the balance idea could not have impressed Moscow, which during the Finnish note crisis in 1961 was told that Sweden would remain neutral under all circumstances. According to the other school of thought, Baltic security would be enhanced by Finnish and Swedish membership in NATO; then NATO's shadow would fall over the Baltic states. Estonia at least would prefer that Finland join NATO. Like Max Jacobson, I support this second thesis that in addition, and primarily, is best for Finland and Sweden.

Vital Interests and Aggression

German strategist Uwe Nerlich has listed three categories of military conflict that NATO needs to be prepared for: major aggression, weapons of mass destruction contingencies, and regional and subregional conflict.[46] How relevant are these categories to Sweden and Finland?

Nerlich argues that major aggression is possible only if the Russian threat is reconstituted. Furthermore, he says, breaches of treaties or agreements, especially CFE and START, will precede any such aggression, as will prior attacks on intermediate countries. Among NATO members, Norway could actually be attacked before any intermediate country. But for the other NATO members Nerlich's assumption is true; to reach Germany you have to cross Poland, and the road to Turkey goes through Armenia.

Nerlich's argument is not true, however, for the Baltic states and Finland. Major aggression against these nations could come as a bolt from the blue, even if the solid Finnish defense makes such a scenario implausible. The Baltic states do form a litmus test: aggression against any one of them will be seen by NATO as a prior attack on an intermediate country and will lead to a reconstitution of the defense effort within the NATO framework.

As late as 1992 Swedish planners envisaged a scenario where a surprise strategic attack could decapitate their nation. But the Russian sealift and airlift for such an operation no longer exists. Now Sweden, like NATO, thinks in terms of a reconstituted threat and focuses on the time frame in which such a threat could again materialize. Although the declared intention is to rebuild the military forces when such a threat is discovered, it is unlikely that the politicians would make timely decisions. More likely Sweden, like Finland, would try to join NATO.

The possibility of the use of weapons of mass destruction (WMDs) is new in European security. The most likely scenarios for WMDs would involve Middle East/Magreb nations or groups attacking Mediterranean nations, e.g., Israel, Turkey, Greece, Italy, France, Spain, or Portugal, to mention just those in the Western camp. Of these nations all but Israel are NATO members and all but Israel and Turkey belong to the EU. Among the Nordic nations WMD contingencies have so far been downplayed because the most likely culprits are far away. However, in addition to the dangers generated by the general post-Soviet environment (listed in appendix 1), Russian, Ukrainian, or minority terrorist groups in East-Central Europe might have access to WMDs. With the continuous decline of Russian conventional forces even Russia itself will put greater emphasis on nuclear weapons, even if it is highly unlikely that even an authoritarian regime would use them first against Europeans. In the face of Russian WMDs, only U.S. nuclear deterrence will work for European nations (with the exception of France and the U.K., which could rely on their own nuclear deterrent).

On a global level the proliferation of WMDs is fought by various arms control regimes. Here, the Nordic nations participate with uneven results in existing regimes such as the Nonproliferation Treaty, the Biological and Chemical Weapons Conventions, the Australia Group, the Missile Technology Control Regime, and so on. Due to its neutral history, Sweden has developed a special capability in fighting the proliferation of WMDs. Although the original purpose of this effort was to maintain its neutrality and independence, the skills developed over time are now a strategic asset for Sweden in its integration into the Western security regime.

As members of NATO and the EU the Nordic nations are expected to act in solidarity if their Southern allies and friends are exposed to WMDs, as is the most likely case. The exact responses that would be made in such a situation are still not worked out within NATO, and have not even been contemplated in the EU.[47] Clearly the military response would come from NATO, while the diplomatic-political-economic response would come from the EU. In August 1995 President Jacques Chirac stated that France could respond to a WMD attack with its own nuclear weapons.[48] France and Germany, in particular, are planning a version of a ballistic missile defense in the long run. For the time being a theater missile defense provided by U.S. forces out of area could shield European troops deployed with the Americans, but this issue now emerges only from one contin-

TABLE 3.5
NATIONAL INTERESTS OF THE NORDIC STATES

Type	Interest
Vital	The defense of the nation and the Nordic neighbors
	U.S. presence in Europe
	The preservation of a viable NATO
Important	The security of the Baltic states and Poland
	The cohesion and integrity of the EU
	The expansion of the EU to include Central Europe and the Baltic states
General	Peace, liberty, and prosperity in Europe, including Russia
	The worldwide nonproliferation of WMDs

gency to another. There is no overall plan for the missile defense of Europe, let alone Northern Europe, in sight.[49]

Regional and subregional conflicts will be the most frequent and likely conflicts in Europe in the years to come. Conflicts in Croatia, Bosnia, Nagorno-Karabakh, Moldova, and Chechnya have already erupted, and it is easy to predict conflicts between Hungary and Romania, Greece and Turkey, or Russia and Ukraine in the future. Whether it is possible and suitable to intervene in such conflicts will be decided by NATO on an ad hoc basis.

James Thomson of RAND makes a distinction between vital, important, and general interest.[50] Table 3.5 shows the interests of the four Nordic nations broken down according to Thomson's scheme. Like other European nations, the Nordic countries must spend resources in order to achieve these goals. In principle the goals of Sweden and Finland are the same as Norway and Denmark.

Notes

[1]Ronald D. Asmus, Richard L. Kugler, and F. Stephen Larrabee, "NATO Expansion: The Next Steps," *Survival* 37:1 (Spring 1995), 10.

[2]*Study on NATO Enlargement* (Brussels: NATO, September 1995).

[3]Ronald D. Asmus, Richard L. Kugler, and F. Stephen Larrabee, "What Will NATO Enlargement Cost?" *Survival* 38:3 (Autumn 1996), 5–26.

[4]The defense committee had to make do with a briefing by former undersecretary of state Sverker Åström. See *Anteckningar från en föredragning*

inför försvarsberedningen av ambassadör Sverker Åström den 20 april 1995. Should Finland consider joining NATO, Sweden should initiate discussions on security cooperation between the Nordic nations to keep them out of the crises that could envelop the continent, claims Åström (p 11).

[5]Arto Nokala, "Finland's Security Policy '95: Consolidation and Main Discussion," in *Yearbook of Finnish Foreign Policy 1995* (Helsinki: Finnish Institute of International Affairs, 1996), 15.

[6]Mauro Mantovani, *NATO-Mitglied Schweiz? Voraussetzungen und folgen einer sicherheitspolitischen integration der Schweiz* (Zürich: Eidgenössische Technische Hochschule, Forschungstelle für Sicherheitspolitik und Konfliktanalyse, 1994).

[7]The new Swiss Army concept "Heere 2000" makes the brigades de facto NATO compatible.

[8]Reich Reiter, *NATO-Beitritt Österreichs?* (Wien: Landesverteidigungsakademie, December 1995) 99–100.

[9]Catherine McArdle Kelleher, *The Future of European Security* (Washington, DC: Brookings, 1995), 64–5.

[10]*Opinion 96* Stockholm: Styrelsen för psykologiskt försvar, November 1996, table 29.

[11]Nils Gyldén, *Sweden's Security and Defence Policy* (Stockholm: Ministry of Defence, 1994), 20–21. The study is *Had There Been a War: Preparations for the Reception of Military Assistance 1949–1969*, SOU 1994:11 (Stockholm: Prime Minister's Office, 1994).

[12]The North Atlantic Treaty was for the first time published in Sweden as Appendix 5 to the official national security report of the defense committee in May 1995, *Sverige i Europa och världen*.

[13]Philip Zelikow, "The Masque of Institutions," *Survival* 38:1 (Spring 1996), 14.

[14]Geir Lundestad, *America, Scandinavia and the Cold War, 1945–1949* (Oslo: Norwegian University Press, 1980); Magne Skodvin, *Norge eller NATO? Utenriksdepartementet og allianssporsmålet 1947–1949* (Oslo: Norwegian University Press, 1971).

[15]*Had There Been a War*, 191.

[16]The cooperation between Finland and Sweden in military intelligence was interrupted neither by World War II nor by the cold war.

[17]*Sydsvenska Dagbladet*, July 20, 1992, 2.

[18]Risto Hyvärinen, Paavo Laitinen, and Ilkka Pastinen, "Suomen turvallisuus muuttuvassa maailmassa," [Finnish Security in a Changing World] *Kanava* 2 (1996), 70–4. Wilhelm Agrell discusses the issue briefly in *Alliansfri—tills vidare* (Stockholm: Natur och Kultur, 1994), Chap. 8.

[19]Iver B. Neumann "Konklusjon. Sikkerhetspolitisk samarbeid som nordisk samarbeid etter den nordlige EU-utvidelse," in Iver B. Neumann, ed., *Ny giv for nordisk samarbeid?* (Oslo: TANO, 1995), 247–8. In April 1996 Neumann proposed an integrated Nordic peacekeeping force and joint military command structure for Norway, Sweden, and Finland, excluding Denmark. See "Bör vi få fellesnordisk militaerkommando?" *Aftenposten*, April 15, 1996.

[20]In 1995 the Danish EU security council published a book designed to ease membership into the WEU. *Dansk og europaeisk sikkerhed* (Copenhagen: SNU, 1995).

[21]Christoph Bertram claims that the nations were told by the United Kingdom and the United States not to apply for WEU membership. Sweden denies that there was a diplomatic intervention. Bertram, *Europe in the Balance* (Washington, DC: Carnegie, 1995), 83.

[22]Robert P. Grant, "France's New Relationship with NATO," has already been overtaken by events. *Survival* 38:1 (Spring 1996), 58–80.

[23]Bertram, *Europe in the Balance*, 77.

[24]*Economist*, February 25, 1995, 19.

[25]The new French defense plan was introduced in a speech by the French president on February 23, 1996. See *Une Défense nouvelle 1997–2015* (Paris: Ministère de la défense, 1996).

[26]Stefan Silvestri, Nicole Gnesotto, and Alvaro Vasconselos, "Decision Making and Institutions," in Lawrence Martin and John Roper, eds., *Towards a Common Defence Policy* (Paris: Institute for Security Studies, 1995).

[27]*Memorandum on the United Kingdom Government's Approach to the Treatment of European Defence Issues at the 1996 Inter-Governmental Conference* (London: FCO, 1996).

[28]*The IGC and the Security and Defence Dimension: Towards an Enhanced EU Role in Crisis Management* (Helsinki and Stockholm: Ministry for Foreign Affairs, April 25, 1996), point 9.

[29]The strongest statement is *A European Union Capable of More Effective Action in the Field of Foreign and Security Policy* (Bonn: Executive Committee of the CDU/CSU Parliamentary Group for the Intergovernmental Conference in 1996, June 1995).

[30]Karl Kaiser, "Challenges and Contingencies for European Defence Policy," in Martin and Roper, eds., *Towards a Common Defence Policy*, 30–1.

[31]One exception was a conference at Ebenhausen in 1995 reported by Suzanne Crow. See *Uniting Europe: EU's and NATO's Expansion and the Future Political Organisation of Europe*, (Ebenhausen: Stiftung Wissenschaft und Politik, April 1995), 27–9.

[32]Anatol Lieven, *The Baltic Revolution* (New Haven: Yale University Press, 1993), 316.

Several new studies concentrate on the Baltic region and thereby advocate regionalization. See John Fitzmaurice, *The Baltic: A Regional Future?* (London: Macmillan 1992); Axel Krohn, *Eine neue Sicherheitspolitik für den Ostseeraum* (Opladen: Leske & Budrich, 1993); Sverre Jervell, Mare Kukk, and Pertti Jonniemi, eds., *The Baltic Sea Area: A Region in the Making?* (Oslo: Baltic Institute, 1993); Pertti Joenniemi, ed., *Cooperation in the Baltic Sea Region* (London: Taylor and Francis, 1993); Nikolaj Petersen, ed., *The Baltic States in International Politics* (Copenhagen: Danish Institute of International Studies, 1993); Pertti Joenniemi and Carl-Einar Stålvant, eds., *Baltic Sea Politics: Achievements and Challenges* (Stockholm: Nordic Council, 1995); and Olav F. Knudsen and Iver B. Neumann, *Subregional Security Cooperation in the Baltic Sea Area* (Oslo: Norwegian Institute of International Affairs, 1995).

[33] Hans Haekkerup, "Cooperation around the Baltic Sea: Danish Perspectives and Initiatives," *NATO Review* 3 (March 1995), 14–18.

[34] Carl Bildt, "The Baltic Litmus Test," *Foreign Affairs* 73:5 (September–October 1994).

[35] Carl Bildt, "Security in Northern Europe. A Swedish Perspective," in Olav F. Knudsen, ed., *Strategic Analysis and the Management of Power. Johan Jörgen Holst, The Cold War and the New Europe* (London: Macmillan, 1996).

[36] Ronald Asmus and Robert Nurick, "NATO Enlargement and the Baltic States," *Survival* 38:2 (Summer 1996), 134.

[37] Bertram, *Europe in the Balance*, 72.

[38] Carl Bildt, "The Baltic States Belong Inside the Line between NATO and Russia," *International Herald Tribune*, May 6, 1995, 8.

[39] An example is Peter van Ham, ed. *The Baltic States: Security and Defence after Independence* (Paris: Institute for Security Studies, 1995), in which the three authors from the Baltic states discuss widely different subjects. Another is Vidmantas Purlys and Gintautas Vikelis, "Cooperation between the Baltic States: A Lithuanian View," *NATO Review* 5 (September 1995), 22–30.

[40] Support of the Baltic States in FY 1991–95 from Sweden amounted to 757 million SEK: 344 million SEK for Estonia, 167 for Latvia, and 246 for Lithuania. Of this, about 300 million SEK was earmarked for national security. Of the amounts given to Estonia and Lithuania 178 million and 77 million, respectively, were repayments of the gold reserve that Sweden had confiscated during World War II. The three Baltic states received about 1 percent of all Swedish foreign aid during this period. Denmark gave the Baltic states the equivalent of 625 million SEK during the same period: 179 million to Estonia, 218 million to Latvia, and 228 million to Lithuania. *Bistånd i siffror och diagram 1991/92, 1992/93 and 1994/95* (Stockholm: SIDA, various years); and communication from the Danish Ministry of Foreign Affairs, September 1995. 750 million SEK is also the accumulated Swedish cost for the effects of the Chernobyl disaster. *Svenska Dagbladet*, May 10, 1996.

[41] Aaron and Regina Karp, *Securing the Baltic: The Politics of Regional Security Cooperation in the Baltic Sea Region* (Norfolk, VA: Old Dominion University, 1996).

[42] Siegfried Thielbeer, "Klare Worte an die Baltische Republiken," *Frankfurter Allgemeine Zeitung*, June 20, 1995.

[43] Douglas Hurd, *Alistar Buchan Memorial Lecture*, International Institute for Strategic Studies, London, March 28, 1996.

[44] Asmus and Nurick, "NATO Enlargement."

[45] Ibid, 133. An earlier version of the text read, "Some observers in Sweden and Finland might feel some discomfort about the prospect of finding themselves in the same category of the Baltic states for fear that this implies a step down in their status as opposed to a step up in the status of the Baltic states. Nevertheless the consolidation of the independence of the Baltic states and their integration into Western structures is a top national security interest of these countries." After intervention from me, among others, the text was changed and the placement of Sweden, Finland, and the Baltic states in the same category was deleted.

[46]Uwe Nerlich, *NATO's Future Functions: Structures and Outreach. Eighth Review of Future Tasks of the Alliance* (Ebenhausen: Stiftung Wissenschaft und Politik, March 24–26, 1995), 32.

[47]Gregory L. Schultz, "Responding To Proliferation: NATO's Role," *NATO Review* (July 1995), 15–18; Robert Joseph, "Proliferation, Counter-Proliferation, and NATO," *Survival* 38:1 (Spring 1996), 111–30.

[48]David S. Yost, "France's Nuclear Dilemma," *Foreign Affairs* 70:1 (January/February 1996), 115.

[49]Sweden has studied the issue of ABM. See Erland Tarras-Wahlberg, Eric Sjöberg, et al., *Skydd mot ballistiska robotar* (Stockholm: FOA, November 1995).

[50]James A. Thomson, *Paper for the American-German conference*, Konrad-Adenauer Stiftung, Sankt Augustin, February 7, 1995.

Conclusion

In 1989 President Bush had promised to keep substantial U.S. nuclear and conventional forces stationed in Europe. His administration believed strongly that, even if the immediate military threat from the Soviet Union diminished, the United States should maintain a significant military commitment in Europe for the foreseeable future. The administration held this view because the political situation seemed so turbulent and unsettled, because U.S. forces in Europe had become vital to projections of American power in other areas such as the Middle East, and because Soviet military power would inevitably remain large enough to overawe Western Europe if the Americans departed. Every European head of government Bush spoke to wanted U.S. forces to stay in Europe, and to stay in strength. The American troop presence thus also served as the ante to ensure a central place for the United States as a player in European politics. The Bush administration places a high value on retaining such influence, underscored by Bush's flat statement that the United States was and would remain "a European power."[1]

This attitude, as described by Philip Zelikow and Condoleezza Rice, has set the stage for European security for many years to come.

In the introduction I raised two questions: Will the Nordic nations become part of the hierarchy of Western political, economic, and military power led by the United States, Germany, the UK and France? and Will military power be readied or employed to influence political developments in or near Europe, especially when the interests of the great powers are not fully engaged? The answer to both questions is "yes", and the answer does not differ from one Nordic nation to another. The two formerly neutral members of the EU, Finland and Sweden, do not reach a different conclusion than do the NATO members Denmark and Norway. Although the form of their policies has differed, the substance is the same.

Since the ability to sustain a modern war is at the heart of European security policy, another of Zelikow's prophesies is pertinent:

> No European country is likely alone to be able to mount a major unilateral conventional campaign outside its homeland (or for some countries even in their homeland) capable of defeating an adversary that can conduct modern military operations. European countries must therefore plan to fight a war that might involve such adversaries only as part of a coalition. The coalition must be more than political; it must integrate individually fragile and unbalanced national armed forces into a stronger whole, employing national specialisation and divisions of labour. Without such a coalition, national armies will not only fight less effectively—they may be unable to fight sustained modern battles at all.[2]

The Nordic nations are the ones that can no longer mount campaigns in their homeland to defeat an adversary that can conduct modern military operations. The only such adversary is potentially Russia (if not now, then maybe in ten years). Leaving out the nuclear equation, which by itself argues for NATO membership, Norway and Denmark drew this conclusion as early as 1949. Finland could not and Sweden would not draw the same conclusion, but now the nature of modern battle has changed and their lonely fight against an able adversary would be doomed from the beginning. Furthermore, they would no longer be able to stay out of a war in Northern Europe. Technology has made geography smaller; the whole Baltic Sea area is a single theater of operation in any scenario larger than limited aggression against the small Baltic states ("limited" on a European scale, but total for the victims).

The nuclear umbrella that was provided by the United States during the cold war has faded into the background; it has been exchanged for an information umbrella. Experiences in Bosnia have taught Sweden and Finland the advantages of access to American dominant battlespace knowledge, whether in the form of intelligence collection, surveillance, and reconnaissance (ISR), C^3I, or precision force—and the disadvantage of being denied such knowledge. To the modernizing air forces of both nations the information umbrella is as attractive as it is necessary. Norwegian and Danish access to NATO advanced warning and control system (AWACS) information is an obvious but pertinent example of what Finland and Sweden currently lack. The wait for a European alternative, currently heralded by France and Germany, is too long, too expensive, offers no political advantage, and is not possible for these nations, which cannot join the WEU without joining NATO at the same time. With highly developed telecommunication systems and world-class corporations—Ericsson and Nokia—Sweden and Finland are eminently fit to develop this force multiplier together with the United States.

Sweden and Finland have demonstrated their commitment to the Western hierarchy of power and the Western security regime and their commitment to use military power if necessary. They have also recognized that it is impossible for a small state to prevail alone against a big modern adversary in war. What has not yet been grasped by everyone in the Finnish and Swedish leadership and public is the insight that it is impossible to stay outside a modern war begun in Northern Europe. Old thought patterns die hard.

The question of political influence in Europe is better understood in these nations. Finland in its excellent national security report in 1995 frequently referred to its role in the EU as a defining one. The Swedish government has proclaimed again and again that it wants to give European policy a Nordic dimension. But as long as these two nations are shut out of the transatlantic dialogue (one of the four main functions of NATO), they will remain marginalized. NATO membership is the *lingua franca* of European security policy; if you do not speak it, people will not hear you.

Membership in the EU is a necessary but not sufficient condition for Nordic security. The eastward expansion of the Western security regime will take place via both the EU and NATO. But a country can control and influence only the organizations that it belongs to, and if a country's arguments in the EU become too tortuous, it risks being ignored by the more important security institution that will go forth anyhow. At the present time Sweden and Finland are treated as models for the East European nations that want to join NATO. Politely it is implied that their membership in the PFP has eased the way for Russian acceptance of the new Western security regime. But they have put themselves on the receiving end of such patronizing comments. Sweden and Finland may be taken more seriously if they change their attitudes.

There is another risk of being marginalized in European security. After thirty years of Gaullism, France has returned to the mainstream of the Western alliance. The civilian triumph of Germany, the forbidding cost of defense, the leadership of the United States, and the end of the cold war are the reasons. But if France is to be the leader in Europe's military partnership with America, it is important for the Nordic nations to understand French motives, resources, and aspirations. If they are not shared, ignorance is a poor base from which to oppose them. Knowledge will bring the insight that many goals are shared—in fighting WMDs, in conducting international operations, and in developing advanced equipment.

For the four Nordic states, the issue comes down to the transatlantic relationship.[3] But Washington is now the capital of the world's only superpower and it is not easy to get the attention of a machine with such far-flung commitments.[4] Nothing will bore an American decisionmaker more than the ritual repetition of neutralist dogma.

In a Europe still of important, if not vital, interest, both Southern and Central Europe remain of interest to the United States. In the Mediterranean the Middle East, Israel, oil, terrorism, fundamentalism, and the threat of WMDs are the focus of American attention. The Sixth Fleet, bureaucratically protected by the U.S. Navy, will remain in place. In Central Europe the issue of NATO expansion and the status of the most powerful European nation, Germany, will keep America involved there. In the North, the strategic nuclear relationship with Russia, symbolized by the Kola complex is of concern to the United States, but this can be handled between Washington and Moscow without any consideration of the local geography and its inhabitants. Hence NATO expansion in the North is the best way to keep Washington focused on the area.

The Western security regime was established by the Bush administration when the cold war ended. In deeds if not yet in words all Nordic nations have joined that regime, have been willing to use force, and have become gradually integrated in its institutions. Unable to meet an adversary (Russia) alone and unable to stay out of a potential war in Northern Europe, these nations should join NATO, which even in peacetime will provide a vital information umbrella in addition to collective security. To wield influence in Europe commensurate with their achievements they need to belong to NATO as well as the EU. To avoid marginalization in European security all the Nordic nations need to understand and appreciate the position of France, the leading future power in the European pillar of NATO. Last but not least, to sustain the interest of America in European security the Nordic nations have to do their share, and joining NATO is the best way to achieve that goal.

Prominent strategists who for tactical reasons shun the concept of NATO speak instead of Nordic defense arrangements of various kinds. In a time of peace and prosperity it is easy to be too clever by half, to be tactical when strategy is required. The time to act is when the conditions are favorable, not when the tide has turned and the competition for security favors is prohibitive. Even in the modern world it takes time to build trust. "A state that is regarded as a good, credible and loyal ally will have greater chances to receive extensive and effective help," says Norwegian historian Olav Riste about the Norwegian predicament in the 1990s.[5] It is time for Finland and Sweden to put their considerable security talents to work in a way that gives them credit.

Notes

[1] Philip Zelikow and Condoleezza Rice, *Germany Unified and Europe Transformed* (Cambridge: Harvard University Press, 1995), 189. As late as 1993 John Lukacs was wrong about the demise of the United States. See Lukacs, *The End of the Twentieth Century and the End of the Modern Age* (New York: Ticknor & Fields, 1993), 109.

[2] Philip Zelikow, "The Masque of Institutions" *Survival* 38:1 (Spring 1996), 12. The theme of invincible American superiority in military technology is

developed by Joseph S. Nye and William A. Owens, "America's Information Edge," and Eliot A. Cohen, "A Revolution in Warfare," in *Foreign Affairs* 75:2 (March/April 1996), 20–36.

[3]Stephen A. Cambone, "The Implications of US Foreign and Defense Policy for the Nordic-Baltic Region," in Den M. Snider and Arne Olav Brundtland, eds., *Nordic-Baltic Security: An International Perspective* (Washington, DC: Center for Strategic and International Studies, 1994).

[4]Richard E. Neustadt, *Alliance Politics* (New York: Columbia University Press, 1970), 78. This theme interested me already in *Arms Deal*, 207.

[5]Olav Riste, *Eit minimumforsvar for Norge?* (Oslo: Institutt for forsvarsstudier, 5 1992), 8. Riste quotes Arne Ording, writing to the Norwegian London government in July 1940: "If the Norwegian government does her utmost to mobilize her material and moral resources for the common cause, Norway's case will rest much stronger."

Appendix

Post-Soviet Crisis Types and Their Nordic Spillover Potential

	Likelihood	Potential Nordic spillover
The "poverty gap"		
Russia muddling down	Ongoing	Conventional pollution and chronic radioactive pollution of various degrees
		Petty crime and smuggling
		Spread of organized crime
		Low-level migration and refugees
		Limited spread of local epidemics in Russia
Russian internal collapse	High	Conventional pollution
		Increased danger of severe radiation pollution
		Spread of organized crime
		Refugee movements of varying intensity, including possible massive flow
		Greater spread of epidemics
Violent conflict in northwest Russia	Possible	Serious danger of severe radiation pollution
		Refugee movements of varying intensity, including possible massive flow
		Inadvertent spillover of fighting
		Use of nuclear weapons or nuclear terror
Political Hardening		
Military-industrial regime	High	Increased international tensions
		Greater Russian pressure on the "near abroad"
		Greater Russian tension in the north
Zhirinovsky-type regime	Possible	Unpredictable political confrontations
		Increasing domestic turmoil
The "Near Abroad"		
Russian pressure on the Baltic states	Possible	Increased Russo-Nordic political tensions
		Refugee flows
		Spillover of fighting or military operations
		Nuclear terror

Source: Tomas Ries, *North Ho: The New Nordic Security Environment and the European Union's Northern Expansion* (Konrad Adenaver Stiftung, Sankt Augustin, November 1994), 29.

Index

References to tables are printed in italics.